Editors

Melissa Hart, M.F.A.

Sara Connolly

Managing Editor

Ina Massler Levin, M.A.

Illustrator

Sue Fullam

Cover Artist

Brenda DiAntonis

Art Production Manager

Kevin Barnes

Imaging

Rosa C. See

Publisher

Mary D. Smith, M.S. Ed.

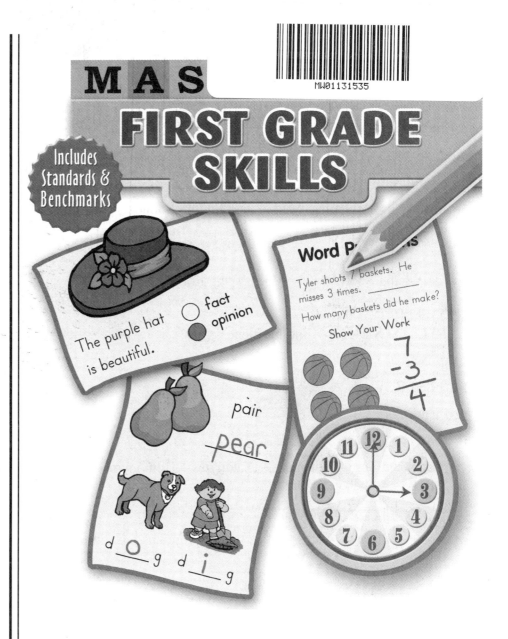

MAS
FIRST GRADE SKILLS

Includes Standards & Benchmarks

Author

Jodene Lynn Smith, M.A.

Teacher Created Resources, Inc.

6421 Industry Way

Westminster, CA 92683

www.teachercreated.com

ISBN 13: 978-1-4206-3956-8

©2006 Teacher Created Resources, Inc.

Reprinted, 2006

Made in U.S.A.

Table of Contents

Table of Contents *(cont.)*

Introduction

The wealth of knowledge a person gains throughout his or her lifetime is impossible to measure, and it will certainly vary from person to person. However, regardless of the scope of knowledge, the foundation for all learning remains constant. All that we know and think throughout our lifetimes is based upon fundamentals, and these fundamentals are the basic skills upon which all learning develops. *Mastering First Grade Skills* is a book that reinforces a variety of fundamentals:

- **Language Arts**
- **Math**
- **Social Studies**
- **Science**

This book was written with the wide range of student skills and ability levels of first grade students in mind. Both teachers and parents can benefit from the variety of pages provided in this book. Parents and children can use the book as an introduction to new material or to reinforce familiar skills. Similarly, a teacher can select pages that provide additional practice for concepts taught in the classroom. When tied to classroom instruction, pages from this book offer homework reinforcement. The worksheets provided in this book are ideal for use at home as well as in the classroom.

Research shows us that skill mastery comes with exposure and drill. To be internalized, concepts must be reviewed until they become second nature. Parents can supplement the classroom experience by exposing children to necessary skills whenever possible, and teachers will find that these pages perfectly complement their classroom curriculum. An answer key beginning on page 230 provides teachers, parents, and children with a quick method of checking responses to completed work sheets.

Basic skills are utilized every day in untold ways. Make the practice of them part of your children's routine. Fundamentals gained now will benefit them throughout their lives.

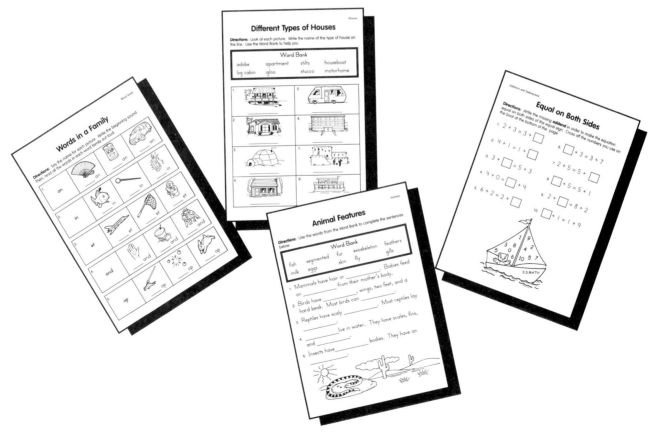

Meeting Standards

Each lesson in *Mastering First Grade Skills* meets one or more of the following standards, used with permission from McREL (Copyright 2000, McRel, Mid-continent Research for Education and Learning. Telephone: 303-337-0990. Website: *www.mcrel.org.*)

Language Arts Standards	Page Number
Uses grammatical and mechanical conventions in written compositions	
• Uses complete sentences in written compositions	79-86, 88-95
• Uses declarative and interrogative sentences in written compositions	84–86
• Uses conventions of spelling in written compositions (e.g., spells high frequency, commonly misspelled words from appropriate grade-level list; spells phonetically regular words; uses letter-sound relationships; spells basic short vowel, long vowel, r-controlled, and consonant blend patterns; uses a dictionary and other resources to spell words; spells own first and last name)	18, 23-25
• Uses conventions of capitalization in written compositions	75–78
• Uses conventions of punctuation in written compositions	72–74
• Uses nouns in written compositions	59–61, 67–68
• Uses verbs in written compositions	62–63, 68
• Uses adjectives in written compositions	64–66, 68, 87
Uses the general skills and strategies of the reading process	
• Uses basic elements of phonetic analysis (e.g., common letter/sound relationships, beginning and ending consonants, vowel sounds, blends, word patterns) to decode unknown words	8–17, 19-22, 26–41, 43–44
• Uses basic elements of structural analysis (e.g., syllables, basic prefixes, suffixes, rootwords, compound words, spelling patterns, contractions) to decode unknown words	42, 45 54–55, 69–71
• Understands how print is organized and read	56–58
• Uses meaning clues (e.g., pictures, picture captions, title, cover, headings, story structure, story topic) to aid comprehension and make predictions about content (e.g., action, events, character's behavior)	46–53, 99
Uses reading skills and strategies to understand and interpret a variety of literary texts	
• Uses reading skills and strategies to understand a variety of familiar literary passages and texts (e.g., fairy tales, folktales, fiction, nonfiction, legends, fables, myths, poems, nursery rhymes, picture books, predictable books)	96, 98, 100, 102–103, 105–107
• Makes simple inferences regarding the order of events and possible outcomes	97, 104
• Knows the main ideas or themes of a story	101

Meeting Standards *(cont.)*

Mathematics Standards	Page Number
Uses a variety of strategies in the problem-solving process	
• Draws pictures to represent problems	138, 150
• Understands and applies basic and advanced properties of the concepts of numbers	
• Counts whole numbers (i.e., both cardinal and ordinal numbers)	108–113, 127–28
• Understands basic whole number relationships (e.g., 4 is less than 10, 30 is 3 tens)	114–126 129–133, 136
• Understands the concept of a unit and its subdivision into equal parts (e.g., one object such as a candy bar, and its division into equal parts to be shared among four people)	185–187
Uses basic and advanced procedures while performing the process of computation	
• Adds and subtracts whole numbers	137–147,149–155 158–159
• Solves real-world problems involving addition and subtraction of whole numbers	134–135, 148 156–157 197–198
• Understands basic estimation strategies (e.g., using reference sets, using front-end digits) and terms (e.g., "about," "near," "closer to," "between," "a little less than")	
• Understands the inverse relationship between addition and subtraction	162–163
• Understands and applies basic and advanced properties of the concepts of measurement	
• Understands the basic measurements of length, width, height, weight, and temperature	174–179
• Understands the concept of time and how it is measured	168–172
• Knows processes for telling time, counting money, and measuring length, weight, and temperature, using basic standard and non-standard units	164–167, 173
• Understands and applies basic and advanced properties of the concepts of geometry	
• Understands basic properties of (e.g., number of sides, corners, square corners) and similarities and differences between simple geometric shapes	182–184 188–189
• Understands the common language of spatial sense (e.g., "inside," "between," "above," "below," "behind")	180–181
• Understands and applies basic and advanced concepts of statistics and data analysis	
• Understands that observations about objects or events can be organized and displayed in simple graphs	193–196
• Understands and applies basic and advanced properties of functions and algebra	
• Extends simple patterns (e.g., of numbers, physical objects, geometric shapes)	190–192

Meeting Standards *(cont.)*

Social Studies Standards	Page Number
Understands and knows how to analyze chronological relationships and patterns	
• Knows how to develop picture time lines – of their own lives or their family's history	217
• Distinguishes among broad categories of historical time (e.g., long, long ago; long ago; yesterday; today; tomorrow)	218
• Knows the English colonists who became revolutionary leaders and fought for independence from England	212
Understands how individuals have worked to achieve the liberties and equalities promised in the principles of American democracy and to improve the lives of people from many groups	
• Understands how important figures reacted to their times and why they were significant to the history of our democracy	212–213, 216
• Knows the history of American symbols	211, 214–215
• Understands and knows how to analyze chronological relationships and patterns	95
• Knows how to develop picture time lines – of their own lives or their family's history	217
• Distinguishes among broad categories of historical time (e.g., long, long ago; long ago; yesterday; today; tomorrow)	218
• Understands how democratic values came to be, and how they have been exemplified by people, events, and symbols	212–216
• Knows the English colonists who became revolutionary leaders and fought for independence from England	212–216
• Understands how individuals have worked to achieve the liberties and equalities promised in the principles of American democracy and to improve the lives of people from many groups	212–216
• Understands how important figures reacted to their times and why they were significant to the history of our democracy	212–213, 216
• Knows the history of American symbols	211, 214–215
Science Standards	**Page Number**
Understands atmospheric processes and the water cycle	228
• Knows that short-term weather conditions (e.g.,) temperature, rain, snow) can change daily, and weather patterns change over the season.	199–200, 229
Understands family life now and in the past, and family life in various places long ago.	
• Know the cultural similarities and differences in clothes, homes, food, communication, technology, and cultural traditions between families now and in the past.	201
• Know the characteristics and uses of maps, globes, and other geographic tools and technologies.	202–210
Understands that scarcity of productive resources requires choices that generate opportunity costs.	197-198
• Knows that goods are things that people make or grow that can satisfy people's needs and wants, and services are jobs people perform that can satisfy peoples needs and wants.	219
Understands the structure and function of cells and organisms	
• Knows the basic needs of plants and animals (e.g., air, water, nutrients, light or food, shelter)	224
• Knows that plants and animals have features that help them live in different environments	222-227
• Understands the structure and properties of matter	220-221

Beginning Sounds

Directions: Say the name for each picture. Write the letter for its beginning sound.

1.	2.	3.	4.
5.	6.	7.	8.
9.	10.	11.	12.
13.	14.	15.	16.

Which Beginning Sound?

Directions: Say the name for each picture. Fill in the bubble that shows the letter for the beginning sound.

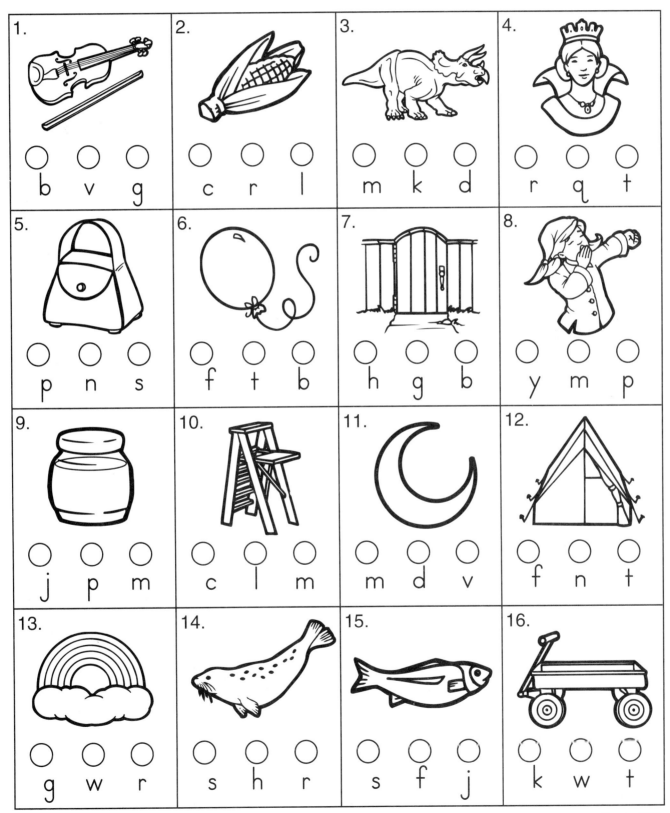

1. ◯ ◯ ◯
   b v g

2. ◯ ◯ ◯
   c r l

3. ◯ ◯ ◯
   m k d

4. ◯ ◯ ◯
   r q t

5. ◯ ◯ ◯
   p n s

6. ◯ ◯ ◯
   f t b

7. ◯ ◯ ◯
   h g b

8. ◯ ◯ ◯
   y m p

9. ◯ ◯ ◯
   j p m

10. ◯ ◯ ◯
    c l m

11. ◯ ◯ ◯
    m d v

12. ◯ ◯ ◯
    f n t

13. ◯ ◯ ◯
    g w r

14. ◯ ◯ ◯
    s h r

15. ◯ ◯ ◯
    s f j

16. ◯ ◯ ◯
    k w t

Change the Sound

Directions: Change the letters that make the beginning sound to form new words. Write the new words on the lines.

1. Change | fan | to _____

2. Change | cat | to _____

3. Change | pen | to _____

4. Change | jet | to _____

5. Change | wig | to _____

6. Change | fin | to _____

7. Change | top | to _____

8. Change | hug | to _____

Change the Beginning Sound

Directions: Change the beginning sound of the underlined word to make a new word which completes each sentence. Use the correct word from the box.

1. The <u>cat</u> wore a _____.

2. The _____ went for a <u>jog</u>.

3. We had <u>fun</u> in the _____.

4. What did you _____ in the <u>net</u>?

5. The <u>dad</u> was very _____.

6. A _____ had a <u>fan</u>.

7. The <u>pig</u> began to _____.

8. There were _____ <u>men</u>.

sun
get
sad
dig
dog
man
ten
hat

Add an Ending Sound

Directions: Say the name for each picture. Write the letter for its ending sound.

1.

su ____

su ____

5.

ma ____

ma ____

2.

pi ____

pi ____

6.

do ____

do ____

3.

we ____

we ____

7.

bu ____

bu ____

4.

ca ____

ca ____

8.

ba ____

ba ____

12

Beginning and Ending Sounds

Directions: Say the name for each picture. Write the letters for its beginning and ending sound.

1.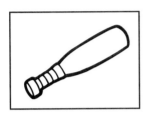

___ a ___

2.

___ i ___

3.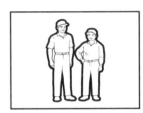

___ e ___

4.

___ u ___

5.

___ o ___

6.

___ a ___

7.

___ o ___

8.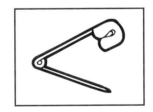

___ i ___

9.

___ u ___

10.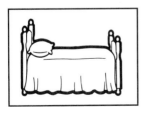

___ e ___

11.

___ a ___

12.

___ o ___

Which Position?

Directions: Name each picture. Listen for the sound at the beginning of each row. If you hear the sound at the beginning of the word, fill in the first bubble. If you hear the sound in the middle of the word, fill in the second bubble. If you hear the sound at the end of the word, fill in the third bubble.

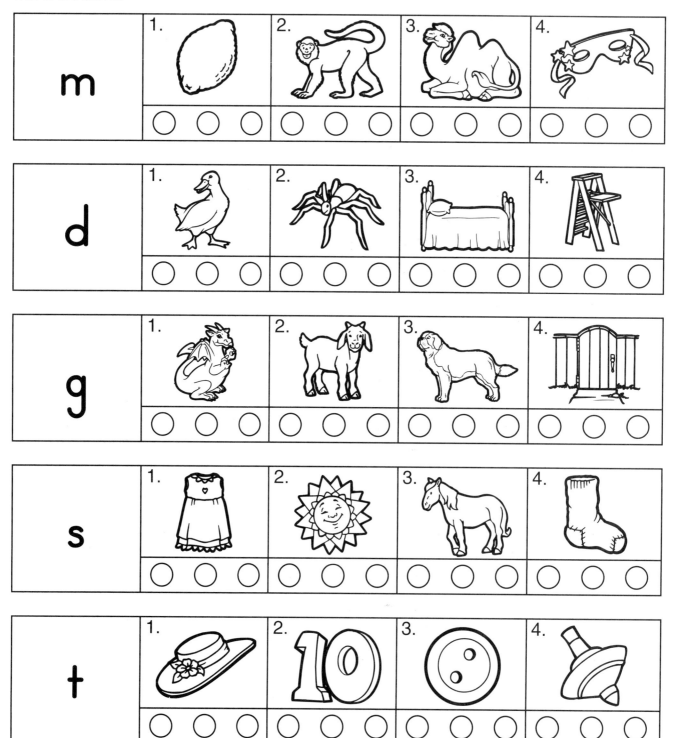

Middle Sounds

Directions: Say the name for each picture. Write the letter for its middle sound.

1.

f ___ n   f ___ n

2.

c ___ t   c ___ t

3.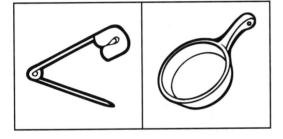

p ___ n   p ___ n

4.

m ___ p   m ___ p

5.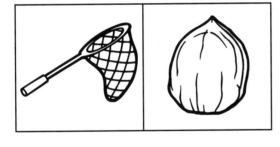

n ___ t   n ___ t

6.

d ___ g   d ___ g

7.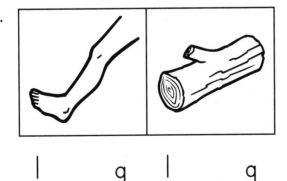

l ___ g   l ___ g

8.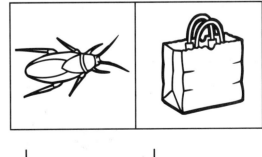

b ___ g   b ___ g

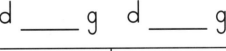

Unscramble the Words

Directions: Read each sentence below. Rearrange the mixed-up letters in the box on the right to make a word that completes the sentence. Write the word on the line.

1.	He has a _____.	act
2.	The pig is in the _____.	mdu
3.	She has _____ eggs.	etn
4.	We got in the _____.	vna
5.	The boy will _____.	tis
6.	She has a _____.	mpa
7.	The _____ can fly.	etj
8.	His job is to _____.	mpo

Where in the Word?

Directions: Use every word in the box to complete the chart below. Find the words that have the beginning, middle, and final consonant of that specific letter. Write the words in the correct column.

gift	play	gum	jar	apple
ring	eggs	milk	nut	ladder
bus	rain	lid	leaf	vest
duck	cup	sack	fall	camel

	Beginning Consonant	Middle Consonant	Final Consonant
d			
f			
m			
n			
p			
s			

Beginning to End

Directions: Say the name for each picture. Unscramble the letters to write the word shown in each picture.

1. t, p, o

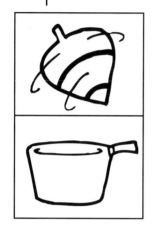

2. g, m, u

3. t, n, e

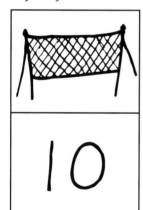

4. p, n, a

5. b, t, a

6. b, s, u

Add a Letter

Directions: Add the letter in the circle to the word shown in the picture to form a new word.

1. (s) +  wing = _____

2. (t) +   wig = _____

3. (c) +  lock = _____

4. (s) + lip = _____

5. (b) +   ring = _____

6. (s) +  pot = _____

7. (b) +  rain = _____

8. (s) +   top = _____

Delete a Letter

Directions: Say the name for each picture. Delete the beginning sound of each word. Write the new word.

1.  boat

2. 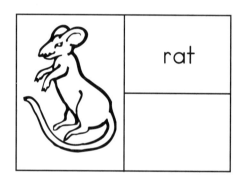 rat

3. 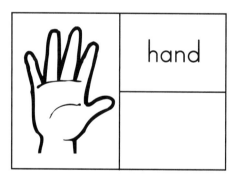 hand

4. 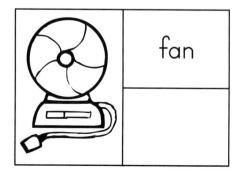 fan

5.  witch

6. 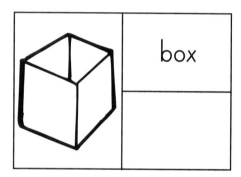 box

7.  fin

8.  mice

Short "Aa" Crossword

Directions: Complete the crossword puzzle by writing **short Aa** words in the correct places. Use the words at the bottom of the page to help you.

Across

2.    3.    4.    5.

Down

1.

2.

3.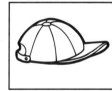

4.

Directions: Trace the short **Aa** words.

Short "Ee" Pictures

Directions: Say the name for each picture. If the word has the **short e** sound, write the letter **Ee** on the line. Color the **short Ee** pictures.

Crossing Short "Ii" Words

Directions: Print the missing letters in the boxes to make short **Ii** words that name each picture.

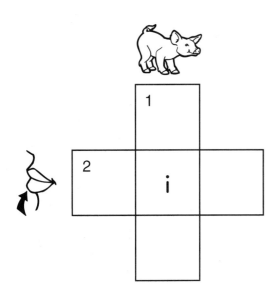

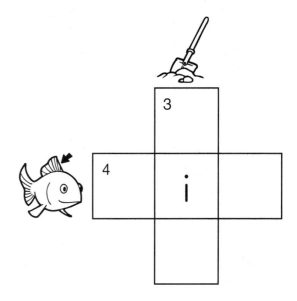

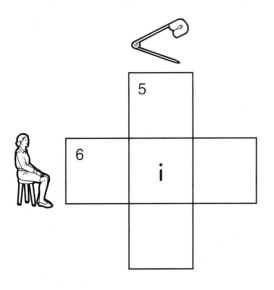

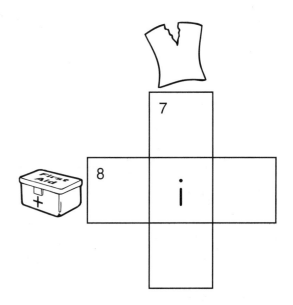

Short "Oo" Words

Directions: Write the name of each picture below. Then, circle the letter that represents the **short Oo** sound.

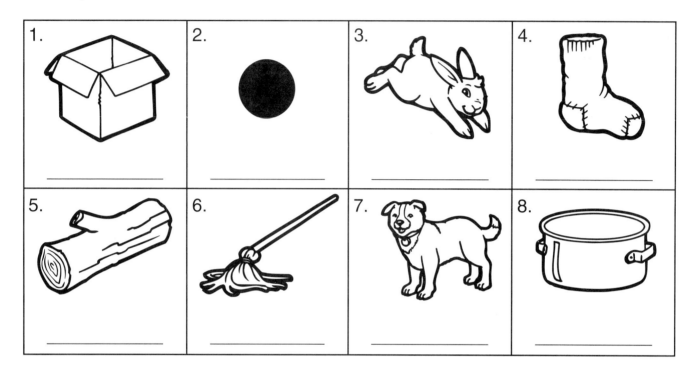

Directions: Study the words above. Now, print a word from above that rhymes with each word below in the spaces provided.

9. top _____

10. hot _____

11. dock _____

12. frog _____

13. hog _____

14. pop _____

15. fox _____

16. got _____

Short "Uu" Word Search

Directions: Write the name of each picture with the **short Uu** sound. Then, find and circle each word in the word search.

1.

2.

```
s   u   n   r   s   b
j   l   t   u   m   u
u   t   u   g   u   g
g   u   b   v   g   n
l   g   e   b   u   n
r   u   n   o   k   p
g   I   c   w   h   d
d   o   f   s   u   b
c   u   b   l   g   c
```

3.

4.

5.

6.

7.

8.

9.
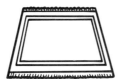

10.

11.

12.

Short "Aa," "Ii," and "Uu"

Directions: Read each word in the first column. Change the **short Uu** to **short Aa**. Write the new word in the second column. Then, change the **short Aa** to **short Ii**. Write the new word in the third column.

Short **Uu** Word	Short **Aa** Word	Short **Ii** Word
1. dud		
2. hum		
3. slum		
4. bun		
5. but		
6. pun		
7. fun		
8. bug		
9. rug		
10. lump		

Directions: Sort the words below into the correct short vowel column.

bad   can
hit   fat
nut   twig
jam   cub
drip   win
run   plug

Short "Aa"	Short "Ii"	Short "Uu"

Which Short Vowel?

Directions: Read each sentence. Circle the word that completes the sentence and write it on the line.

	1. The dog sat in the _____ .	set sun sick
	2. The pig is on the _____ .	mop map mat
	3. The bug is in the _____ .	top net nest
	4. I put him in the _____ .	tub tan top
	5. The _____ is in the mud.	cot cub can
	6. He can _____ .	dig den dot
	7. A fish has a _____ .	fat fin fell
	8. The egg came from the _____ .	hen hot hip

Long "Aa"

Directions: Read the word in the first column that describes the item. Look in the second column for a rhyming word. Print the answer in the third column.

cage	cape	wait	bake
tail	paid	hay	face

	Clue	Rhyme	Answer
1.	a dog has one of these	rhymes with **mail**	
2.	you do this to a cake	rhymes with **lake**	
3.	Superman wears one	rhymes with **tape**	
4.	a hamster is kept in this	rhymes with **rage**	
5.	you do this in line	rhymes with **bait**	
6.	a horse eats it	rhymes with **say**	
7.	you have to work to get this	rhymes with **maid**	
8.	this is part of your head	rhymes with **race**	

Long "Ee"

Directions: Read the sentences below and follow the directions.

1. Draw a **bee** on a **leaf**.	2. Draw **three trees**.
3. Draw a **seal** in a **jeep**.	4. Draw a **beet**, **bean**, and **pea**.
5. Draw an **eel** In the **sea**.	6. Draw a **deer** at the **beach**.

Long "Ii"

Directions: Read the word on the left. Draw a line to the picture on the right that matches the word.

1. tire

2. bike

3. pie

4. night

5. dime

6. five

7. tie

8. mice

Long "Oo"

Directions: Say the name of each picture. Color the boxes that contain a word that rhymes with the name of the picture.

1.

stone	boat	tone	alone
rose	cone	ban	throne

2.

low	to	mow	loan
mine	snow	tow	row

3.

moat	coat	vote	toad
boat	dot	float	cut

4.

bold	fold	folk	cold
toad	told	hold	hand

Long "Uu"

Directions: Complete each sentence below by writing the word that names the **long Uu** picture.

| duet | flute | Utah | uniforms | tuba | June | tune |

1. Next _____ the band will go on a trip.

2. They will travel to _____.

3. The band will wear their new _____.

4. Jewel will be playing the _____.

5. Raul will play the _____.

6. The band will play a happy _____.

7. Sue and Jude will sing a _____.

Magic "Ee"

Directions: Say the name for each picture. Write the correct **short** or **long** vowel word that names the picture. Use the words from the box below.

1.

_____

2.

_____

3.

_____

4.

_____

5.

_____

6.

_____

7.

_____

8.

_____

9.

_____

10.

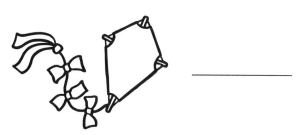

_____

Word Bank				
can	kitc	tap	tube	kit
tub	cub	cane	cube	tape

Short or Long?

Directions: Say the name for each picture. Print the vowel sound that you hear on the line. If the vowel is **short**, fill in the bubble labeled **short**. If the vowel is **long**, fill in the bubble labeled **long**.

1.	2.	3.	4.
____ ○ short ○ long	____ ○ short ○ long	____ ○ short ○ long	____ ○ short ○ long
5.	6.	7.	8.
____ ○ short ○ long	____ ○ short ○ long	____ ○ short ○ long	____ ○ short ○ long
9.	10.	11.	12.
____ ○ short ○ long	____ ○ short ○ long	____ ○ short ○ long	____ ○ short ○ long
13.	14.	15.	16.
____ ○ short ○ long	____ ○ short ○ long	____ ○ short ○ long	____ ○ short ○ long

Long and Short Vowel Train Cars

Directions: Write the name of each picture in the correct train car matching the vowel sound. The first one has been done for you.

1. Long Aa — cake   Short Aa — cat

2. Long Ee   Short Ee

3. Long Ii   Short Ii

4. Long Oo   Short Oo

5. Long Uu   Short Uu

         #3956 Mastering First Grade Skills

Long and Short Vowel Sort

Directions: Read the words below. Listen for the **long** or **short** vowel sound. Write the words in the correct column.

suit	yet	plug	juice	cut
cab	stub	fed	boat	leap
best	dock	plan	fog	take
stick	bride	grape	line	snap
blame	spot	green	rip	eel
like	woke	swing	note	glue

Short Aa	Short Ee	Short Ii	Short Oo	Short Uu
Long Aa	Long Ee	Long Ii	Long Oo	Long Uu

"Rr," "Ll," and "Ss" Blends

Directions: Say the name for each picture. On the line, write the blend you hear at the beginning of the word.

Sorting "Rr," "Ll," and "Ss" Blends

Directions: Read each word. Divide the words by blend. Write each word in the correct column. Circle the blend.

dragon	globe	star	swim	spider	stop
swing	frame	present	crown	truck	block
plant	bridge	clap	smoke	glue	crib
stone	clam	sponge	play	grape	flame

Rr blends	Ll blends	Ss blends

Blends

Ending Blends

Directions: Say the name for each picture. Find the word that names the picture. Write it beside the picture. Underline the ending blend.

skunk   mask   blimp   desk   lamp   ring   plant

fist   jump   tusk   stamp   wink   film   east

1. _____	2. _____
3. _____	4. _____
5. _____	6. _____
7. _____	8. _____
9. _____	10. _____
11. _____	12. _____
13. _____	14. _____

Identifying Digraphs

Directions: Read the word in the first column. Write the digraph in the second column. Fill in the bubble in the third column to show if the digraph is heard at the beginning, in the middle, or at the end of the word.

Digraphs			
ch	sh	th	wh

Word	Digraph	Position in Word		
		Beginning	Middle	End
1. cherry	ch	●	○	○
2. match		○	○	○
3. father		○	○	○
4. mouth		○	○	○
5. wash		○	○	○
6. lunch		○	○	○
7. sheep		○	○	○
8. teacher		○	○	○
9. whale		○	○	○
10. three		○	○	○
11. with		○	○	○
12. wheel		○	○	○

Controlled Rr Words

Directions: Say the name for each picture. Print its name under it. Use the list of words to help you. Then, sort the words in the correct columns in the chart below.

star	horse	river	thirteen	tractor	turkey
nurse	corn	bird	shark	letter	yarn

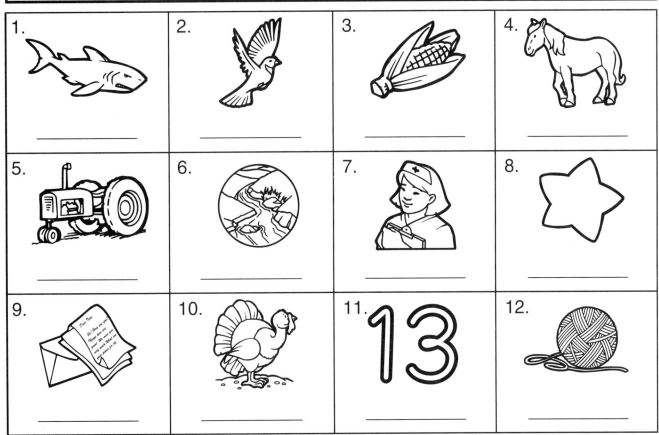

ar	er	ir	or	ur

Word Endings

Directions: Read each word in the first column. Make new words by adding the endings **s**, **ed**, or **ing**. Write the new words in the correct columns.

Base Word	Add "s"	Add "ed"	Add "ing"
1. jump			
2. mow			
3. cook			
4. open			
5. answer			

Directions: Write the base word for each of the words below.

6. picked _____

7. crashed _____

8. smiles _____

9. going _____

10. looking _____

11. helps _____

12. talked _____

13. plays _____

14. loves _____

15. seeing _____

Words in a Family

Directions: Say the name for each picture. Write the beginning sound. Then, read all the words in each word family out loud.

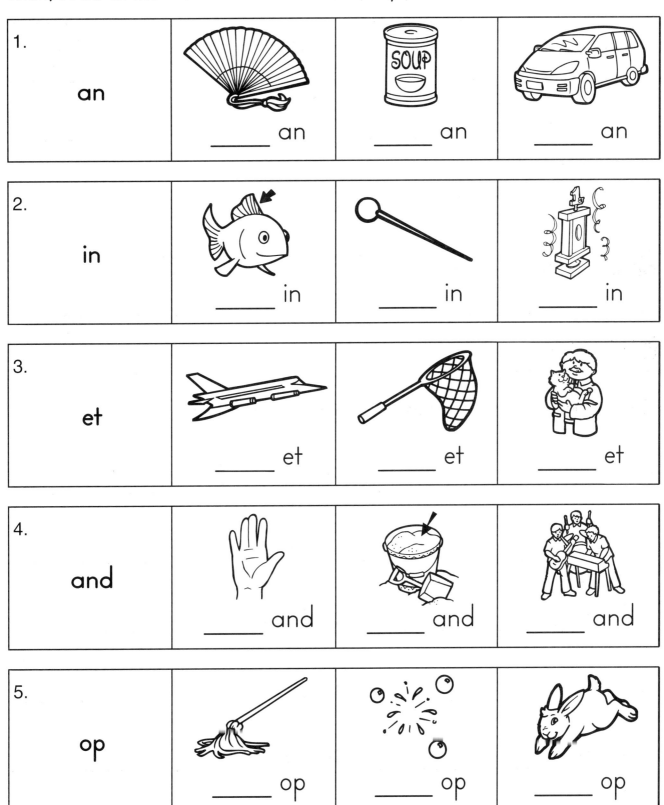

1. an

_____ an _____ an _____ an

2. in

_____ in _____ in _____ in

3. et

_____ et _____ et _____ et

4. and

_____ and _____ and _____ and

5. op

_____ op _____ op _____ op

Rhyming Sentences

Directions: Complete the blank in each sentence with a word that rhymes with the underlined word. Use the words from the Rhyming Word Bank to help you.

Rhyming Word Bank

truck	hat	fish	box
bike	book	bee	frog

1. <u>Look</u> at the _____.

2. The <u>fox</u> is in a _____.

3. On the <u>log</u> sits a _____.

4. The <u>cat</u> wears a _____.

5. There is a <u>duck</u> in my _____.

6. I <u>wish</u> I had a _____.

7. I <u>see</u> a _____.

8. I <u>like</u> my _____.

Sorting Word Families

Directions: Look at each picture. Say the word. Write the word. Then, sort the words into the correct column at the bottom of the page, according to their sound.

1.	2.	3.	4.
5.	6.	7.	8.
9.	10.	11.	12.

−ap	−et	−ot	−ug

Synonym Find

Directions: Read each sentence. Write a synonym on the line for the underlined word in the sentence. Use the words from the Word Bank to help you.

Word Bank			
glad	speak	chilly	home
shut	hog	loud	mad

1. The <u>pig</u> was in the pen. _____

2. I was <u>happy</u> to see my dad. _____

3. It was a <u>cold</u> day. _____

4. <u>Close</u> the door. _____

5. She was <u>angry</u>. _____

6. The baby was very <u>noisy</u>. _____

7. He wants to <u>talk</u> to you. _____

8. The boy went in the <u>house</u>. _____

Antonym Crossword

Directions: Choose the antonym from the Word Bank below that has the opposite meaning as the puzzle clue. Print the word in the correct box.

Clues

Down

1. deep
3. young
6. kind
8. heavy

Across

2. adult
4. boy
5. black
7. come

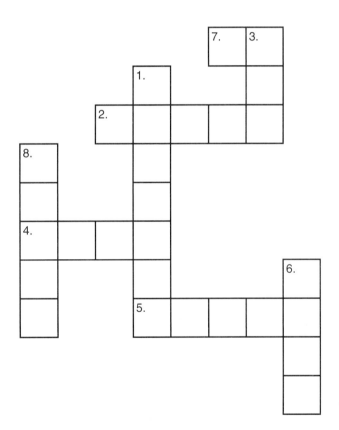

Word Bank

shallow	mean	girl	go
white	child	old	light

Opposite Sentences

Directions: Complete each pair of sentences with words that mean the opposite of each other. Use the Word Bank to help you.

Word Bank

hot	won	up	asleep	big	small
awake	open	lost	cold	close	down

---

1. The cat is _____.

   The cat is _____.

2. _____ the door.

   _____ the door.

3. The soup was _____.

   The soup was _____.

4. Look at the _____ pumpkin.

   Look at the _____ pumpkin.

5. The elevator is going _____.

   The elevator is going _____.

6. We _____ the baseball game.

   We _____ the baseball game.

Synonyms or Antonyms

Directions: Read each pair of words. Decide if the words are **synonyms** or **antonyms**. Fill in the correct bubble.

1. end stop	○ synonyms ○ antonyms	7. wet dry	○ synonyms ○ antonyms
2. uncle aunt	○ synonyms ○ antonyms	8. hurry rush	○ synonyms ○ antonyms
3. start begin	○ synonyms ○ antonyms	9. sink float	○ synonyms ○ antonyms
4. clean dirty	○ synonyms ○ antonyms	10. save keep	○ synonyms ○ antonyms
5. sunny cloudy	○ synonyms ○ antonyms	11. fix break	○ synonyms ○ antonyms
6. pretty ugly	○ synonyms ○ antonyms	12. rough smooth	○ synonyms ○ antonyms

Synonyms and Antonyms Sort

Directions: Read each word. Write a **synonym** and an **antonym** for the word. Use the words from the Word Bank to help you.

Word Bank

ill	smile	large	different	arrive	small
quick	alike	frown	leave	slow	well

Word	Synonym	Antonym
1. sick		
2. same		
3. big		
4. fast		
5. grin		
6. come		

Sounds the Same, Spelled Differently

Directions: Study the word in each box. Then, print a word from the Word Bank that sounds the same as the boxed word but is spelled differently and has a different meaning.

Word Bank

flour	aunt	sale	son	tale	be
right	ate	pear	not	would	to

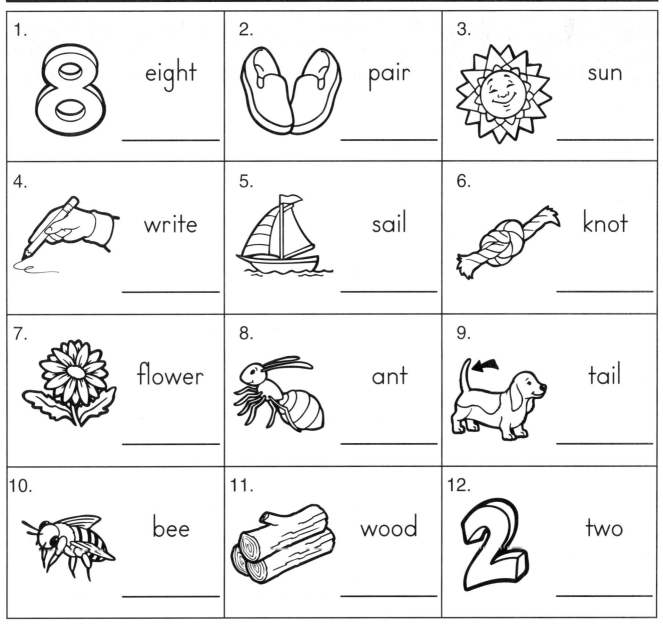

1. eight _____

2. pair _____

3. sun _____

4. write _____

5. sail _____

6. knot _____

7. flower _____

8. ant _____

9. tail _____

10. bee _____

11. wood _____

12. two _____

Homonym Sentences

Directions: Read each sentence. Use the two **homonyms** in the box to the left to complete the sentence.

1. eight ate	He _____ _____ grapes.
2. knead need	I _____ to _____ the dough.
3. tail tale	I wrote a _____ about my dog's _____ .
4. knew new	She _____ I got a _____ car.
5. eye I	_____ got dirt in my _____ .
6. write right	Do you _____ with your _____ hand?
7. four for	I have _____ flowers _____ you.
8. so sew	The button fell off _____ I had to _____ it back on.

Two Meanings

Directions: Look at each pair of pictures. Write a word that names both pictures. Use the words from the Word Bank to help you.

1.  _____

2.  _____

Word Bank

pot

bat

top

saw

bowl

orange

3.  _____

4.  _____

5. 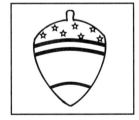 _____

6. 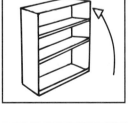 _____

Make a Compound Word

Directions: Look at each picture. Write the words that names the picture. Then, write the words together to make a compound word. Use the Word Bank to help you.

```
┌─────────────────────────────────────────────────────────────────┐
│                         Word Bank                                 │
│                                                                   │
│   house        dog         tea         foot        rain          │
│   ball         pot         shell       bow         sea           │
└─────────────────────────────────────────────────────────────────┘
```

1.  +  = _____

2.  +  = _____

3.  +  = _____

4.  +  = _____

5. 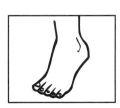 + 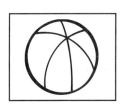 = _____

Compound Word Sentences

Directions: Choose two words in each sentence to put together into a **compound word** to illustrate the picture.

1. A **house** for a **dog** is a _____.

2. A **man** made out of **snow** is a _____.

3. A **shell** from the **sea** is a _____.

4. A **bird** that is **blue** is a _____.

5. A **hive** for a **bee** is a _____.

6. A **bell** for a **door** is a _____.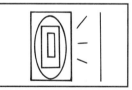

7. A **room** for a **bed** is a _____.

8. A **pot** for **tea** is a _____.

Animal ABC Order

Directions: Put these words in alphabetical order.

1.

cat   dog

lizard   bird

_____

_____

_____

_____

2.

lion   giraffe

tiger   elephant

_____

_____

_____

_____

3.

pig   cow

horse   sheep

_____

_____

_____

_____

4.

fish   crab

octopus   shark

_____

_____

_____

_____

Fruits and Vegetables ABC Order

Directions: Put these words in alphabetical order.

Fruits

banana	orange
plum	apple
pear	cherry

Vegetables

potato	pea
carrot	squash
bean	lettuce

_____

_____

_____

_____

_____

_____

_____

_____

_____

_____

Same Letter ABC Order

Directions: Put these words in alphabetical order.

1.		2.	
doll	_____	gum	_____
dance	_____	gate	_____
drive	_____	glue	_____
dinosaur	_____	goat	_____
deer	_____	grape	_____

3.		4.	
melt	_____	snake	_____
monkey	_____	sail	_____
milk	_____	slide	_____
math	_____	soft	_____
mud	_____	smell	_____

Person, Place, or Thing?

Directions: Read each sentence below. Identify the **nouns** in the sentence. Write the **nouns** on the correct lines.

1. Dad rode a bike to the park.

_____   _____   _____
   person   place   thing

2. The children sang a song at the theater.

_____   _____   _____
   person   place   thing

3. The pool was full of children in bathing suits.

_____   _____   _____
   person   place   thing

4. The queen wore her crown in the castle.

_____   _____   _____
   person   place   thing

5. The boy returned the book to the library.

_____   _____   _____
   person   place   thing

Naming Common Nouns

Directions: Look at each picture in the first column. Read the common noun in the second column. Write a proper noun that names each common noun in the third column. Then, write if the noun is a person, place or thing in the last column.

	Common Noun	Proper Noun	Person, Place, or Thing?
Example:	car	Ford	thing
1.	school		
2.	teacher		
3.	planet		
4.	park		
5.	boy		
6.	month		
7.	doctor		
8.	river		

More Than One

Directions: Write a singular noun for the first picture. Make the noun plural to match the second picture.

	Singular		Plural
Example:	ant		ants
1.			
2.			
3.			
4.			
5.			
6.			
7.			
8.			

Action Words

Directions: Write the word that shows what someone or something does.

1. The dog chased the cat._____

2. The star twinkles in the sky. _____

3. The children watched the parade. _____

4. My brother set the table. _____

5. I swim like a fish. _____

6. The bird sings a pretty song. _____

7. You eat the last piece. _____

8. The player threw the ball._____

Action Sentences

Directions: Write a **verb** for each picture. Then, write a sentence using the **verb**.

	Verb	Sentence
1.		
2.		
3.		
4.		
5.		
6.		

Describe It

Directions: Write a word that describes each picture below. Use the words in the Word Bank to help you.

Word Bank

hot	three	round	smelly
quiet	cute	big	beautiful

1.

_____

- - - - - - - - - - - -

_____

2.

_____

- - - - - - - - - - - -

_____

3.

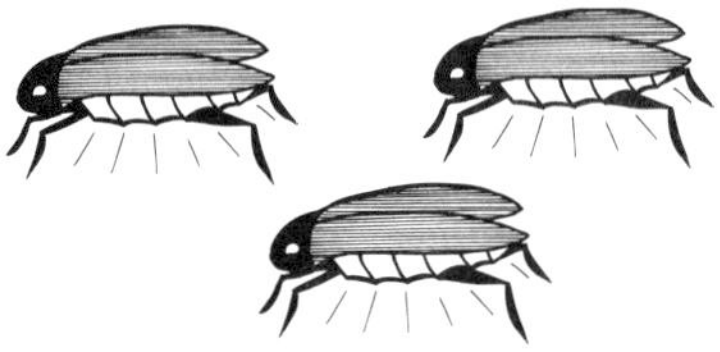

_____

- - - - - - - - - - - -

_____

4.

_____

- - - - - - - - - - - -

_____

5.

SH-SH

_____

- - - - - - - - - - - -

_____

6.

_____

- - - - - - - - - - - -

_____

7.

_____

- - - - - - - - - - - -

_____

8.

_____

- - - - - - - - - - - -

_____

How Many? What Kind?

Directions: Say the name for each picture in the first column. Then, write a word in the second column that describes "how many." Write a word in the third column that describes "what kind."

	How Many?	What Kind?
1.	_____ sun	_____ sun
2.	_____ dogs	_____ dogs
3.	_____ eggs	_____ eggs
4.	_____ boys	_____ boys
5.	_____ bus	_____ bus
6.	_____ apples	_____ apples
7.	_____ books	_____ books
8.	_____ bear	_____ bear

A Descriptive Story

Directions: Use **adjectives** from the Word Bank to add more description to each sentence in the story below. Your sentences can be silly or serious. The words may fit in more than one blank.

Word Bank			
scrambled	red	warm	two
spiky	orange	blue	best

1. This morning I got out of my _____ bed.

2. I went to the bathroom and brushed my _____ hair.

3. I got dressed in pants and a _____ shirt.

4. For breakfast, I ate _____ eggs and _____ pieces of bacon.

5. Then, I drank _____ juice.

6. Finally, my _____ friend and I walked to school.

Pronoun Party

Directions: Rewrite the sentence using a **pronoun** from the Word Bank in place of the underlined noun or nouns.

Word Bank			
it	I	them	they
his	she	we	us

1. My mom drove <u>Jenny, Ester, Emily and me</u> to Max's party.

   _____

2. She didn't mind driving <u>Jenny, Ester, and Emily</u> because she was already taking me. _____

3. <u>Jenny and I</u> bought Max the perfect present. _____

   _____

4. <u>The present</u> was a boomerang. _____

5. <u>Max, Sam, and Andy</u> played with the boomerang until the cake was served. _____

6. Before Max blew out the candles, he put <u>Max's</u> boomerang away.

   _____

7. Mrs. Lucas called us when <u>Mrs. Lucas</u> was ready to light the candles.

   _____

8. I told my mom, "<u>Lisa</u> never had so much fun at a party."

   _____

Parts of Speech Review

Directions: Look at the pictures below. Write each word from the picture in the correct column.

Nouns	Verbs	Adjectives

Which Contraction?

Directions: Read the sentences below. Circle the correct **contraction** on the right to replace the underlined words.

1. <u>I am</u> going to help my mom.	I'll I'm
2. <u>We are</u> going to bake a cake.	We're We've
3. There <u>is not</u> any sugar.	it's isn't
4. You <u>cannot</u> bake a cake without sugar.	can't isn't
5. <u>We will</u> need to go to the store.	We've We'll
6. It <u>should not</u> take long.	shouldn't wouldn't
7. The store <u>is not</u> far away.	isn't can't
8. <u>It is</u> only two blocks.	Isn't It's

Making Contractions

Directions: Read the two words on the leaves of each flower. Write a **contraction** in the center of the flower using the two words from the leaves.

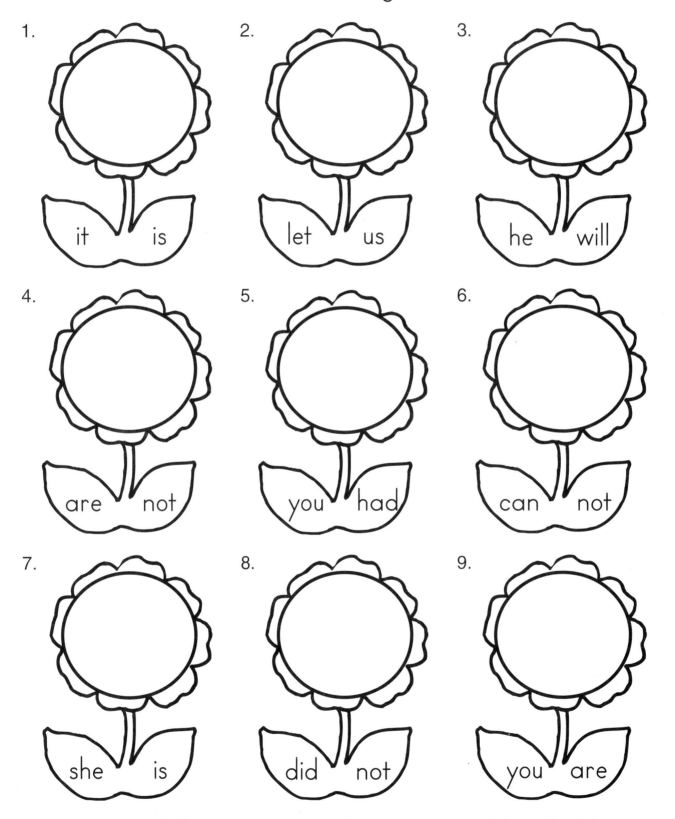

1. it   is

2. let   us

3. he   will

4. are   not

5. you   had

6. can   not

7. she   is

8. did   not

9. you   are

Finding Contractions

Directions: Study the circled contraction in each sentence below. Write the two words that make up the contraction in the columns on the right. The first one has been done for you.

	Word 1	Word 2
1. (It's) very cold outside.	It	is
2. She (couldn't) open the door.		
3. (We're) going to the store.		
4. I think (you'd) like the movie.		
5. Look! (It's) a puppy!		
6. (They're) on the way.		
7. I (can't) come right now.		
8. (He's) my best friend.		
9. (Wouldn't) you like to go too?		
10. (I'm) six years old today.		

Statement or Question?

Directions: Read each sentence below. Decide if the sentence is a **statement** or a **question**. Circle the correct ending punctuation mark.

Example: When is your birthday	.
	(?)
1. My birthday is in June	.
	?
2. I am going to have a party	.
	?
3. Will you be able to come	.
	?
4. We can play games	.
	?
5. My mom will bake a cake	.
	?
6. What is your favorite flavor	.
	?
7. I hope my friends bring presents	.
	?
8. I can hardly wait	.
	?

Write a Question

Directions: Write a question to go with each answer. Don't forget to include a **question mark** at the end of each sentence.

Question	Answer
Example: What animal says, "Oink"?	a pig
1.	red
2.	science
3.	pizza
4.	a bunny
5.	the dentist
6.	my brother
7.	polka dots
8.	swimming

End It Right

Directions: Read each sentence below. Write the correct **punctuation mark** at the end of the sentence.

1. Does your class have a pet

2. My class has a pet lizard

3. His name is Tiny Tim

4. One day the lizard escaped

5. We looked all over the classroom for him

6. Do you know how hard it is to find something so small

7. We looked and looked

8. Then Sandy yelled, "There he is"

9. We put him back in his cage

10. We were so happy

First Words

Directions: Practice capitalizing the first word in each sentence by writing it on the line.

1. _____ mom took me shopping.

    my

2. _____ we play now?

    can

3. _____ like to eat pizza.

    i

4. _____ are going to the movies.

    we

5. _____ helped me bake a cake.

    she

6. _____ are eggs in the nest.

    there

7. _____ you coming with us.

    are

8. _____ favorite color is yellow.

    her

Name It

Directions: Complete each sentence with a **proper noun**. Capitalize each **proper noun**.

1. _____ is now on video.

   (Name of a movie)

2. My favorite cartoon is _____ .

   (Name of a cartoon)

3. Our class sang "_____."

   (Name of a song)

4. _____ is my best friend.

   (Name of a person)

5. My birthday is in _____ .

   (Name of a month)

6. Yesterday was _____ .

   (Name of a day of the week)

7. I like to drink _____ .

   (brand name of a drink)

8. On February 14 we celebrate

   _____ .

   (Name of the holiday)

Where Do You Live?

Directions: Complete each sentence below with a **proper noun** to show the specific place you live. Capitalize each **proper noun**.

1. I live on _____.
   (planet)

2. I live in _____.
   (continent)

3. I live in _____.
   (country)

4. I live in _____.
   (state)

5. I live in _____.
   (city)

6. I live on _____.
   (street)

Directions: Complete the sentence below with the information you wrote in the blanks above.

I live on _____ in _____
            (planet)   (continent)

in _____ in _____
       (country)   (state)

in _____ on _____.
       (city)   (street)

Capitalizing Proper Nouns

Directions: Read each sentence. Underline any word that needs a capital letter. Write the word correctly on the line.

Example:

my family went on vacation. ___My___

1. We went to california. _____

2. Our hotel was called sunshine hotel. _____

3. My favorite day of the trip was tuesday. _____

4. We went to see the pacific ocean. _____

5. My brother and i splashed in the waves. _____

6. My sister sally built a sand castle. _____

7. Dad bought us drinks from the shake shack. _____

8. we had a really great time. _____

Scrambled Sentences

Directions: Put the words below in order to make a sentence.

1. dog so The is cute.

   _____

2. just She puppies had eight.

   _____

3. were two There black puppies.

   _____

4. Five were puppies brown.

   _____

5. last the What was of color the one?

   _____

Complete Sentences

Directions: Read each sentence below. Decide if it is a **complete sentence** or an **incomplete sentence**. Fill in the correct bubble. Rewrite the **incomplete sentences** as **complete sentences** on the lines at the bottom of the page.

1. We were hungry.	○ complete ○ incomplete
2. My mom made us lunch.	○ complete ○ incomplete
3. She made us	○ complete ○ incomplete
4. It was very good.	○ complete ○ incomplete
5. Tomorrow she will make	○ complete ○ incomplete

_____

_____

Writing Complete Sentences

Directions: Choose one word or phrase from each column below to help you write **complete sentences**. Words may be used in more than one sentence.

Who	Did What	Where
My teacher	sang	on our street.
I	laughed	at school.
Sally	ate	in the rain.
The dog	ran	by the tree.

1. _____

2. _____

3. _____

4. _____

Make a Sentence

Directions: Choose one word from each column below to write a complete sentence.

Adjectives	Nouns	Verbs	Adverbs
This	girl	skipped	quietly
The	nurse	read	quickly
One	cat	slept	carefully
A	father	helped	slowly

Example: A girl skipped quickly.

1. _____

2. _____

3. _____

4. _____

Create a Sentence

Directions: Create your own sentences using the words below. You may want to use different forms of the words below, and add other words to your sentences.

1. The dog _____ .

2. The _____ dog _____ .

3. The _____ .

4. The _____ .

5. _____ .

Answer the Question

Directions: Write a complete sentence to answer each question below.

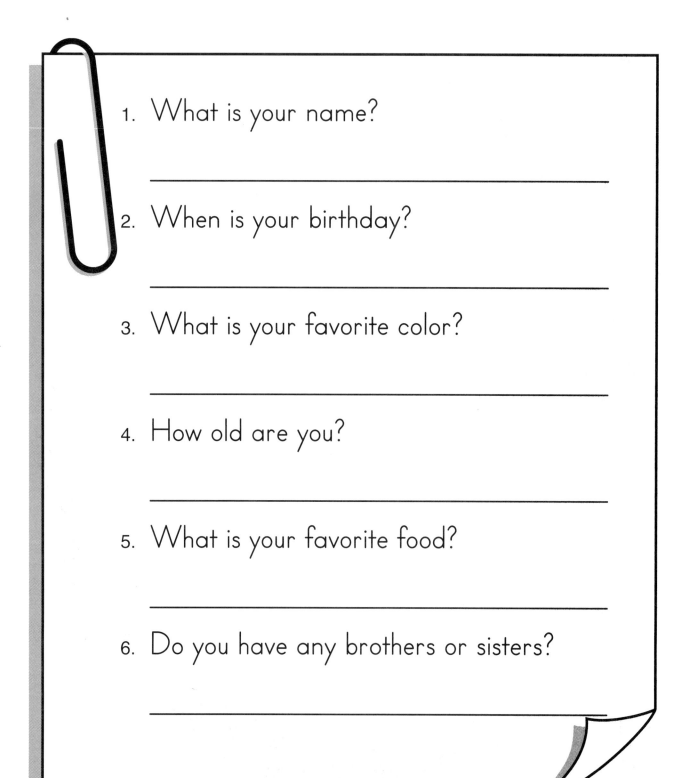

1. What is your name?

   _____

2. When is your birthday?

   _____

3. What is your favorite color?

   _____

4. How old are you?

   _____

5. What is your favorite food?

   _____

6. Do you have any brothers or sisters?

   _____

Changing Questions into Statements

Directions: Change each of the following questions into statements.

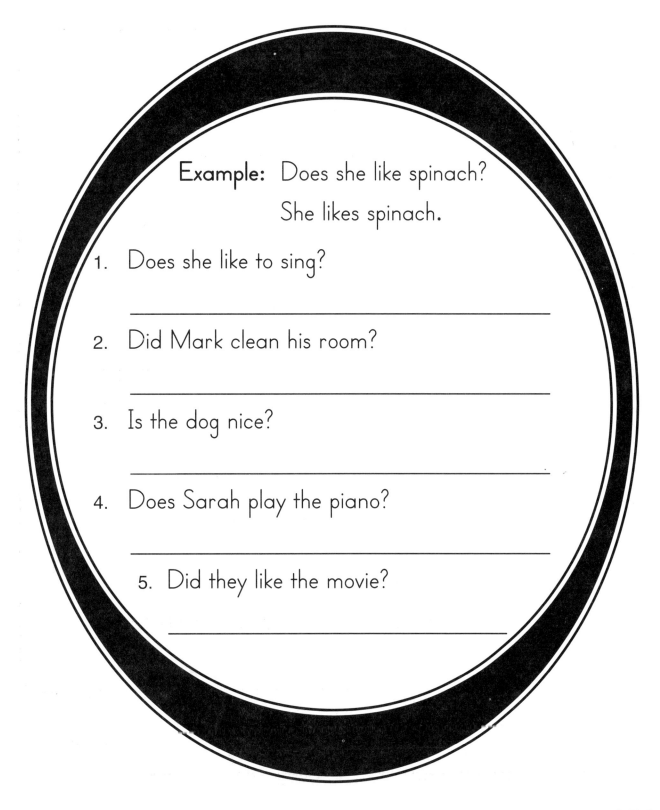

Example: Does she like spinach?

She likes spinach.

1. Does she like to sing?

   _____

2. Did Mark clean his room?

   _____

3. Is the dog nice?

   _____

4. Does Sarah play the piano?

   _____

   5. Did they like the movie?

   _____

Changing Statements into Questions

Directions: Change each of the following statements into questions.

Example: The dog is cute.

Is the dog cute?

1. Mike has three pets.

_____

2. She loves her brother.

_____

3. We had sandwiches for lunch.

_____

4. Mom made cookies for us.

_____

5. Louie likes to do math.

_____

Adding Adjectives to Sentences

Directions: Write a word in each blank to expand the sentence. If you need help, use the Word Bank. Words from the Word Bank may be used in more than one sentence.

1. The _____ dog is cute.

2. Maria read a/an _____ book.

3. Dad mowed the _____, _____ grass.

4. He ran to the _____ house.

5. The lady sang a _____ song.

6. She sat in the _____ chair.

7. The _____ rabbit ate a/an _____ carrot.

8. My uncle has a _____ beard.

Word Bank

little	beautiful	green	white	big
tall	interesting	orange	comfortable	fuzzy

Expanding Sentences

Directions: Practice writing longer sentences by rewriting each sentence. Add at least two more words to make the sentence more interesting.

Example: The dog barked.

The little brown dog barked loudly.

1. She loves to read.

_____

2. Laura has a bike.

_____

3. He is my friend.

_____

4. Do you like cake?

_____

5. My mom made dinner.

_____

Create a Story

Directions: Choose one item from each group to use in a story. You can use other characters, settings, objects, and situations in your story, too.

A.
- ❏ a picnic
- ❏ a parade
- ❏ a field trip
- ❏ a car ride

B.
- ❏ the beach
- ❏ a barn
- ❏ the theater
- ❏ the airport

C.
- ❏ a grandma
- ❏ a fireman
- ❏ a monkey
- ❏ a dad

D.
- ❏ an eraser
- ❏ a tire
- ❏ a banana
- ❏ a tree

What Is It?

Directions: Use your imagination to finish the picture below. Turn your page any way you wish to help you think of ideas. When your picture is finished, write a story about what you have created.

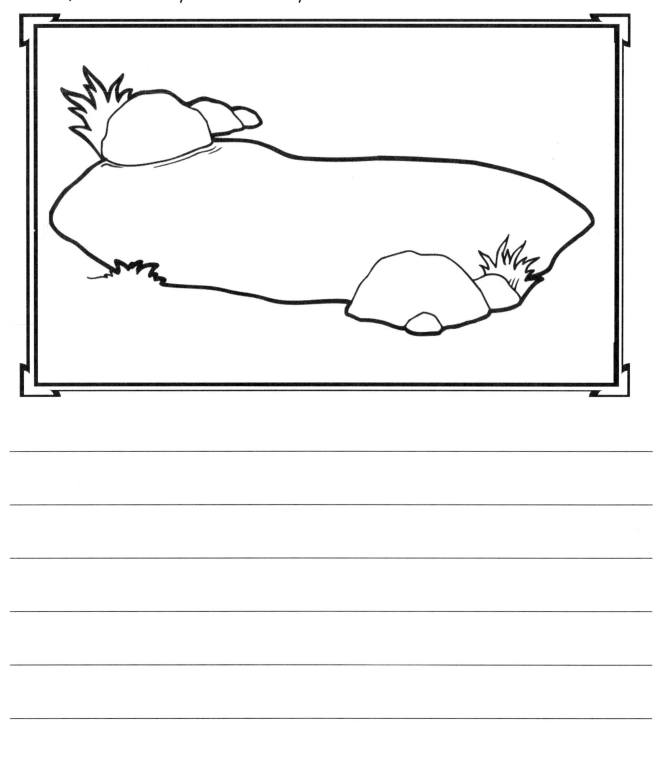

_____

_____

_____

_____

_____

_____

Who Lives Here?

Directions: What kinds of things live in caves? Draw a picture of a creature in the cave below. Write a story about your cave creature.

_____

_____

_____

_____

Marooned

Directions: Write a story using the beginning below.

If I were marooned on an island . . .

_____

_____

_____

_____

_____

Octopus Bath

Directions: Write a story using the beginning below.

One day I came home from school and found an octopus in my bathtub.

_____

_____

_____

_____

_____

Observing a Banana

Directions: Use your five senses to observe a banana. Record your findings on the chart below. Use the chart to help you write about what you observed.

 Banana 				
Sight 	Touch 	Hearing 	Smell 	Taste 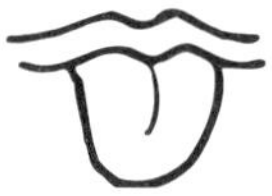

_____

_____

_____

_____

_____

_____

Sequencing Events

Directions: Think about the first actions you took when you got up this morning. Use the organizer below to help you plan your story. Then, write about your morning.

1st action	2nd action	3rd action

_____

_____

_____

_____

_____

_____

Real or Make Believe?

Directions: Read each sentence. Decide if it is real or make believe. Fill in the correct bubble.

1. She had brown hair.	◯ real ◯ make believe
2. He ate one thousand bananas for breakfast.	◯ real ◯ make believe
3. Dad was mowing the lawn.	◯ real ◯ make believe
4. The purple dog ran quickly.	◯ real ◯ make believe
5. The cat barked at the dog.	◯ real ◯ make believe
6. Mary baked a chocolate cake.	◯ real ◯ make believe
7. We had a great time at the party.	◯ real ◯ make believe
8. My brother is 200 years old.	◯ real ◯ make believe

Predicting

Directions: Read each story. Decide what will happen next. Fill in the bubble to show your answer.

1. It is Marie's birthday. Mom is having a birthday party for her. She wrapped a gift and baked a cake. All she has left to do is . . .
   - (a.) go to the bank.
   - (b.) plant some corn.
   - (c.) decorate the house with balloons.

2. It is Mark's job to take care of the dog. Once a week Mark gives the dog a bath. Mark fills the bathtub with water. He scrubs the dog with soap. Finally, he . . .
   - (a.) rinses and dries the dog.
   - (b.) calls his friend on the phone.
   - (c.) walks to school.

3. Sophia loves to bake cookies. Her mom helps her mix the dough. Sophia scoops the dough onto cookie sheets. Then, Sophia . . .
   - (a.) writes a story.
   - (b.) practices the piano.
   - (c.) puts them in the oven.

Fact or Opinion

Directions: Read each statement. Decide if it is a fact or an opinion. Fill in the correct bubble.

1.	There are seven days in a week.	○ fact ○ opinion
2.	The purple shirt is beautiful.	○ fact ○ opinion
3.	A bicycle has two wheels.	○ fact ○ opinion
4.	It is a long walk to school.	○ fact ○ opinion
5.	A dog is the best kind of pet.	○ fact ○ opinion
6.	*The Cat in the Hat* was written by Dr. Seuss.	○ fact ○ opinion
7.	The radio is loud.	○ fact ○ opinion
8.	Thanksgiving is in November.	○ fact ○ opinion
9.	A dime is worth 10 pennies.	○ fact ○ opinion
10.	The rose smells sweet.	○ fact ○ opinion

Word Use

Directions: Read each sentence. Fill in the bubble that tells the meaning of the underlined word in each sentence.

1. Sue made <u>punch</u> to serve at the party.

   (a.) to strike or hit   (b.) sweetened drink

2. My mom had to <u>rock</u> the baby to sleep.

   (a.) mass of stone   (b.) to move back and forth

3. His <u>pupil</u> is learning to play the piano.

   (a.) student   (b.) opening in the iris of the eye

4. We are going to <u>bowl</u> at the birthday party.

   (a.) type of dish   (b.) to roll a ball to hit pins

5. Dad swatted the <u>fly</u> away from his face.

   (a.) small insect   (b.) to move through the air on wings

6. They walked along the <u>bank</u> of the river.

   (a.) steep slope or rising ground   (b.) place for saving and lending money

Sequencing

Directions: Read the sentences. Write them on the lines below in the correct order.

Her wobbly legs pushed her up.

She put her front hooves on the grass.

The new pony lay quietly on the ground.

The new pony was standing on her own!

She lifted her nose into the air.

1. _____

2. _____

3. _____

4. _____

5. _____

Main Idea

Directions: Read the words in each box. Decide on a category for the words. Use the words from the Word Bank.

Word Bank			
colors	clothes	fruit	numbers
instruments	months	seasons	writing tools

1. winter spring summer fall _____	5. pencil crayon marker pen _____
2. apple orange pear banana _____	6. red purple yellow blue _____
3. piano flute drum violin _____	7. one eight four ten _____
4. pants shirt sweater dress _____	8. January July September December _____

Supporting Details

Directions: Write the words from the Word Bank in the correct category.

Shapes	Instruments
_____	_____
_____	_____
_____	_____
_____	_____

Buildings	Transportation
_____	_____
_____	_____
_____	_____
_____	_____

Word Bank

car	library	triangle	motorcycle
bank	ship	school	tuba
piano	violin	plane	rectangle
circle	square	drums	house

Categorizing

Directions: Read the names of the categories in the first column. Think of three words that fit into each category. Write the words in the following columns.

1. Things you can find at the beach			
2. Things you read			
3. Things that move			
4. Things that are hot			
5. Things you play with			
6. Things on a farm			
7. Things in a kitchen			
8. Things at a park			

Inferring

Directions: Read each short story. Fill in the bubbles to show the best answer to the questions.

1. Bob wears a wig. He puts on big shoes and silly clothes. Bob paints his face with make up. Then he goes to work. What is Bob's job?

   (a.) fireman   (b.) clown   (c.) bus driver

2. Sue could hear meowing. She walked over to the tree and looked up. What was in the tree?

   (a.) a bird   (b.) a dog   (c.) a cat

3. Mom did not want to cook dinner tonight. The doorbell rang. A man was standing there with a thin square box. What was for dinner?

   (a.) pizza   (b.) an apple   (c.) cereal

4. Mark drew a shape on his paper. He did not lift his pencil at all. The shape has no straight lines. What shape did Mark draw?

   (a.) square   (b.) circle   (c.) triangle

5. Mary went with her mom to visit family. They visited her mom's mom. Who did Mary see?

   (a.) her sister   (b.) her uncle   (c.) her grandma

Penguins

Directions: Read the passage below. Answer the questions at the bottom of the page by filling in the correct bubble.

Penguins

Penguins are unusual birds. They have feathers, but they cannot fly. They are very good at swimming. In fact, penguins spend most of their time swimming. The water is where penguins find their food. They really enjoy eating fish, squid, and krill. There are not many birds like the penguin!

1. What is a penguin's body covering?

   (a.) fur   (b.) feathers   (c.) scales

2. What are penguins good at?

   (a.) sliding   (b.) swimming   (c.) walking

3. What do penguins like to eat?

   (a.) fish   (b.) insects   (c.) plants

4. What is the main idea of the paragraph?

   (a.) Penguins are good swimmers.

   (b.) Penguins find their food in water.

   (c.) Penguins are unusual birds.

Best Friends

Directions: Read the story below. Answer the questions at the bottom of the page. Use complete sentences.

Best Friends

Martha and Janis are best friends. Every afternoon, the girls do their homework together. They munch on their favorite snack, popcorn. After they finish their homework, Martha and Janis go to the park. Marta takes her skates. She is a great skater. Janis brings her scooter. When Pete comes along, all the children swing and slide. They all enjoy that. It is good to have a best friend.

1. Who are the best friends? _____

2. What do the girls do in the afternoon?

   _____

3. Where do the girls go when they are done with their homework? _____

4. What do the girls do at the park? _____

   _____

5. Who is your best friend?

   _____

Giraffes

Directions: Read the passage below. Answer the questions at the bottom of the page by filling in the correct bubble.

Giraffes

Giraffes live on the grasslands of Africa. They are known for their long legs and necks. Giraffes are so tall that they feed on leaves at the tops of trees. Giraffes use their long tongues to pull the leaves off the trees. In order for giraffes to get water, they have to spread their front legs apart and bend way down low. Although giraffes have few enemies, they are always on the lookout for danger. They have good eyesight and hearing to help them.

1. What are giraffes known for?

   (a.) their patterns   (c.) their good eyesight

   (b.) their long legs and necks

2. What does the word *feed* mean in this passage?

   (a.) eat   (b.) seed   (c.) collect

3. How do giraffes get leaves?

   (a.) from a caregiver   (c.) pull them off the trees

   (b.) collect them on the ground

4. Why do giraffes have to spread their legs when drinking water?

   (a.) their height   (c.) to reach the leaves

   (b.) to look for danger

5. What was the author's purpose in writing this passage?

   (a.) to entertain   (c.) to persuade

   (b.) to inform

Connect the Dots

Directions: Count by connecting the dots in number order.

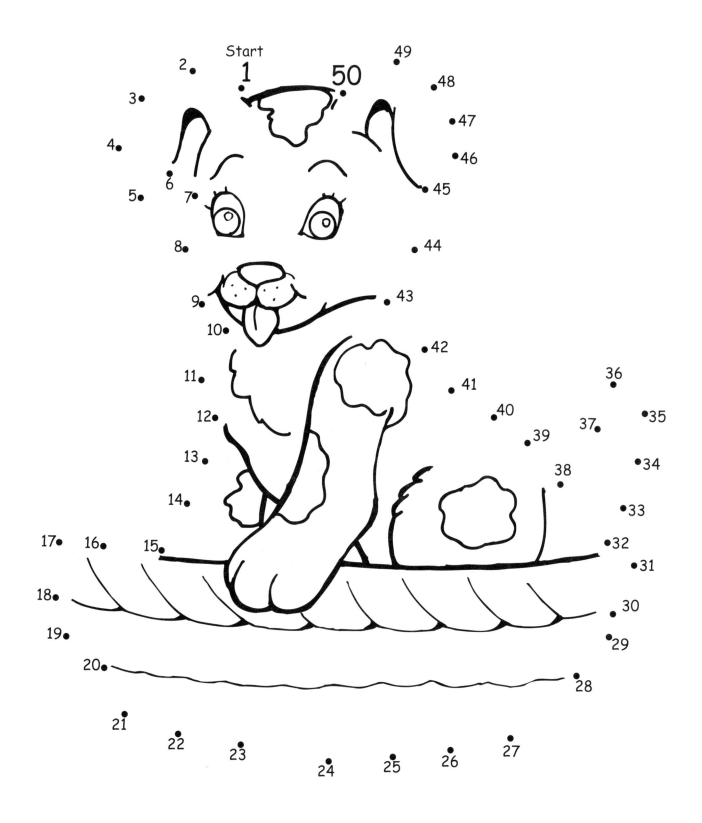

Connect The Dots

Directions: Count by connecting the dots in number order.

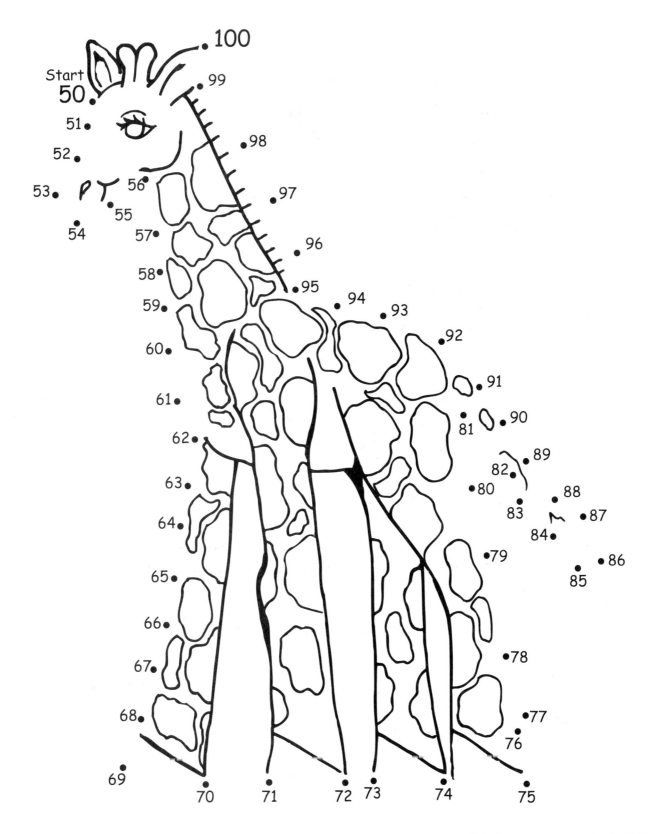

Counting to 100

Directions: Complete the chart by writing in the missing numbers.

1	2								10
		13				17			
				25					
			34				39		
		43							50
					56				
61							68		
	72					77			80
			85						
			94					99	

110

Count, Write, Name

Directions: Count the number of pictures. Write the numeral. Then, write the number name. Use the Word Bank to help you with spelling the number names.

Word Bank				
one	two	three	four	five
six	seven	eight	nine	ten

1.	Numeral		6.	Numeral
	Number Name			Number Name
2.	Numeral		7.	Numeral
	Number Name			Number Name
3.	Numeral		8.	Numeral
	Number Name			Number Name
4.	Numeral		9.	Numeral
	Number Name			Number Name
5.	Numeral		10.	Numeral
	Number Name			Number Name

Number Name Picture

Directions: Read the number name in each space. Color, using the code below, to reveal a hidden picture.

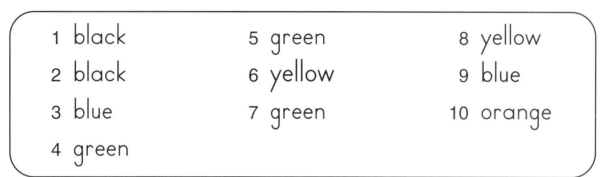

1 black	5 green	8 yellow
2 black	6 yellow	9 blue
3 blue	7 green	10 orange
4 green		

Larger Number Names

Directions: Read the number names. Write the number on the line.

1. seventy-two _____
2. sixteen _____
3. forty-one _____
4. thirty-eight _____
5. twenty-three _____

6. eighty-seven _____
7. four _____
8. fifty-six _____
9. sixty-five _____

Write the numbers from above in order from least to greatest.

____ ____ ____ ____ ____ ____ ____ ____ ____

Connect the dots from least to greatest to make a picture.

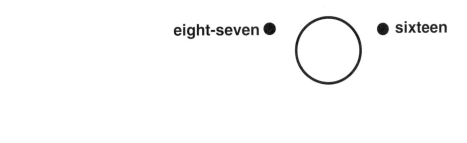

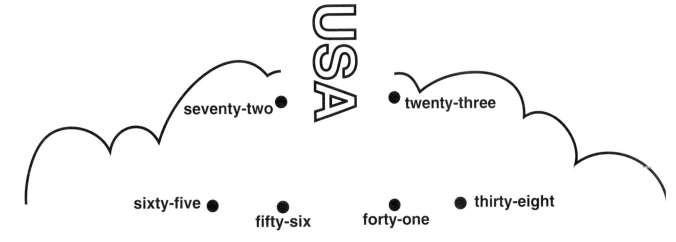

Counting Tens and Ones

Directions: Count the tens and ones. Write the total of each on the small lines. Then, write the sum of both numbers on the large line.

1. _____ tens _____ ones = _____

2. _____ tens _____ ones = _____

3. _____ tens _____ ones = _____

4. _____ tens _____ ones = _____

5. = _____ tens _____ ones = _____

6. _____ tens _____ ones = _____

7. _____ tens _____ ones = _____

8. _____ tens _____ ones = _____

Counting Balls

Directions: Count the tens and ones. Write the correct numbers on the lines.

1. 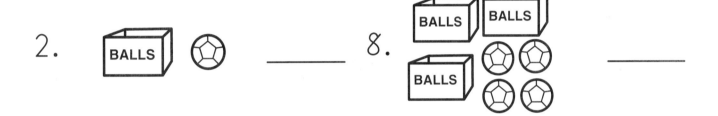 _____

2. _____

3. _____

4. _____

5. _____

6. _____

7. _____

8. _____

9. _____

10. _____

11. _____

12. _____

Writing Numbers in Expanded Notation

Directions: Write each number in expanded notation.

1. $52 = 50 + 2$

2. $47 = \underline{} + \underline{}$

3. $96 = \underline{} + \underline{}$

4. $63 = \underline{} + \underline{}$

5. $39 = \underline{} + \underline{}$

6. $24 \underline{} + \underline{}$

7. $81 \underline{} + \underline{}$

8. $17 \underline{} + \underline{}$

9. $4 \underline{} + \underline{}$

10. $75 \underline{} + \underline{}$

Directions: Look for a pattern. Fill in the lines with the correct number.

11. $50 + 0 = 50$

$50 + 1 = 51$

$50 + 2 = 52$

$50 + \underline{} = 53$

$\underline{} + \underline{} = 54$

$\underline{} + \underline{} =$

12. $70 + 5 = 75$

$70 + 6 = 76$

$70 + 7 = 77$

$70 + 8 =$

$\underline{} + 9 =$

$\underline{} + \underline{} = 80$

Find the Numbers

Directions: Use the clues to circle the correct number or numbers.

1. Circle the numbers that have a **4** in the **tens** place.

   43   29   63   41   78   37   49

2. Circle the numbers that have a **9** in the **ones** place.

   19   97   58   79   63   9   29

3. Circle the number that has **2 tens** and **5 ones.**

   35   57   52   26   25   53   16

4. Circle the numbers that have **no ones.**

   21   60   43   30   76   43   75

5. Circle the numbers that have **no tens.**

   43   7   17   8   2   59   36

6. Circle the number that has a **1** in the **hundreds** place.

   10   61   100   43   90   82   41

7. Circle the numbers that you say when you count by **10s.**

   40   62   90   85   100   34   67

8. Circle the numbers that you say when you count by **5s.**

   5   27   30   43   50   65   72

Make a Number

Directions: Use the two numbers shown to make new numbers. Make the largest number and the smallest number. The first one has been done for you.

1.
5
2
Largest 52
Smallest 25

2.
9
5
Largest ___
Smallest ___

3.
3
6
Largest ___
Smallest ___

4.
7
5
Largest ___
Smallest ___

5.
4
8
Largest ___
Smallest ___

6.
6
9
Largest ___
Smallest ___

7.
1
7
Largest ___
Smallest ___

8.
3
4
Largest ___
Smallest ___

9.
7
9
Largest ___
Smallest ___

10.
8
2
Largest ___
Smallest ___

11.
6
4
Largest ___
Smallest ___

12.
1
8
Largest ___
Smallest ___

13.
7
3
Largest ___
Smallest ___

14.
3
5
Largest ___
Smallest ___

15.
0
5
Largest ___
Smallest ___

Mystery Numbers

Directions: Follow the directions below to make a number.

1. Make a number that has . . .
   a **two** in the **ones** place,
   a **five** in the **tens** place,
   a **nine** in the **hundreds** place.

hundreds	tens	ones

_____

2. Make a number that has . . .
   a **six** in the **ones** place,
   an **eight** in the **tens** place,
   a **one** in the **hundreds** place.

hundreds	tens	ones

_____

3. Make a number that has . . .
   a **three** in the **ones** place,
   a **zero** in the **tens** place,
   a **four** in the **hundreds** place.

hundreds	tens	ones

_____

4. Make a number that has . . .
   a **seven** in the **ones** place,
   a **six** in the **tens** place,
   a **two** in the **hundreds** place.

hundreds	tens	ones

_____

5. Make a number that has . . .
   an **eight** in the **ones** place,
   a **nine** in the **tens** place,
   a **three** in the **hundreds** place.

hundreds	tens	ones

_____

6. Make a number that has . . .
   a **zero** in the **ones** place,
   a **zero** in the **tens** place,
   a **one** in the **hundreds** place.

hundreds	tens	ones

_____

Using Number Clues

Directions: Read the clues. Write the number. Then, write the number name.

Clue	Number	Number Name
Example: four tens and two ones	42	forty-two
1. seven tens and three ones		
2. nine tens and seven ones		
3. three tens and eight ones		
4. six tens and six ones		
5. one ten and four ones		
6. four tens and zero ones		
7. zero tens and five ones		
8. eight tens and one one		
9. two tens and seven ones		
10. five tens and nine ones		

More Number Clues

Directions: Read the clues to determine the correct number. Write it on the line.

1. I am thinking of a number.
   It is **greater** than 21.
   It is **less** than 23.
   What is the number? _____

2. I am thinking of a number.
   It is **less** than 40.
   It is **greater** than 30.
   You say it when you count by **5s**.
   What is the number? _____

3. I am thinking of a number.
   It has a 2 in the **ones** place.
   It has a 7 in the **tens** place.
   What is the number? _____

4. I am thinking of a number.
   It is **less** than 20.
   It has a 0 in the **ones** place.
   What is the number? _____

5. I am thinking of a number.
   It is **less** than 80.

   It is **greater** than 70.
   You say it when you count by **2s**.
   It has a 4 in the **ones** place.
   What is the number? _____

6. I am thinking of a number.
   It is **less** than 10.
   It is **odd**.
   It is **greater** than 7.
   What is the number? _____

7. I am thinking of a number.
   It is **greater** than 50.
   It is **less** than 60.
   It has a 3 in the **ones** place.
   What is the number? _____

8. I am thinking of a number.
   It is an **even** number.
   It has a 4 in the **tens** place.
   It has a 6 in the **ones** place.
   What is the number? _____

Number Gumball Machine

Directions: Color the gumballs using the color code.

1 – 20 Red	61 – 80 Green
21 – 40 Orange	81 – 100 Yellow
41 – 60 Blue	

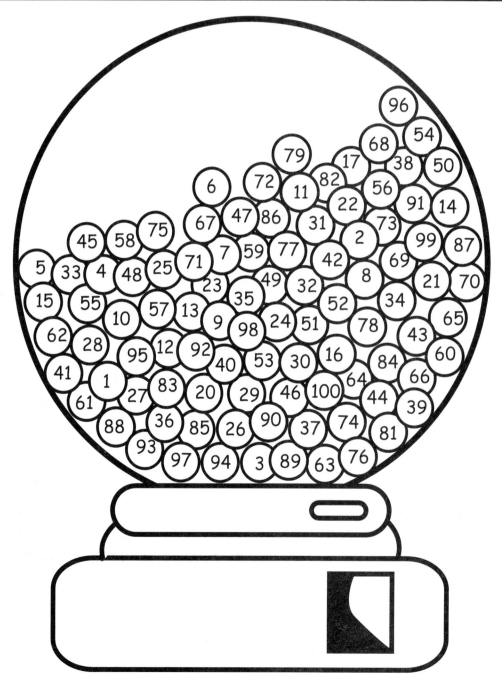

Number Sense

Before, After, Between

Directions: Write the number that comes before.

1. _____ 16   5. _____ 35
2. _____ 29   6. _____ 72
3. _____ 67   7. _____ 53
4. _____ 48   8. _____ 89

Directions: Write the number that comes after.

9. 19 _____   13. 38 _____
10. 93 _____   14. 84 _____
11. 62 _____   15. 55 _____
12. 47 _____   16. 26 _____

Directions: Write the number that comes between.

17. 23 _____ 25   21. 41 _____ 43
18. 56 _____ 58   22. 75 _____ 77
19. 94 _____ 96   23. 87 _____ 89
20. 32 _____ 34   24. 16 _____ 18

Bonus:

What number comes before 80? _____

Sequencing Numbers

Directions: Place the numbers on the berries in order from **least** to **greatest**.

1.

_____ _____ _____ _____ _____

2.

_____ _____ _____ _____ _____

3.

_____ _____ _____ _____ _____

4.

_____ _____ _____ _____ _____

5.

_____ _____ _____ _____ _____

6.

_____ _____ _____ _____ _____

Missing Apartment Numbers

Directions: Fill in the missing apartment numbers.

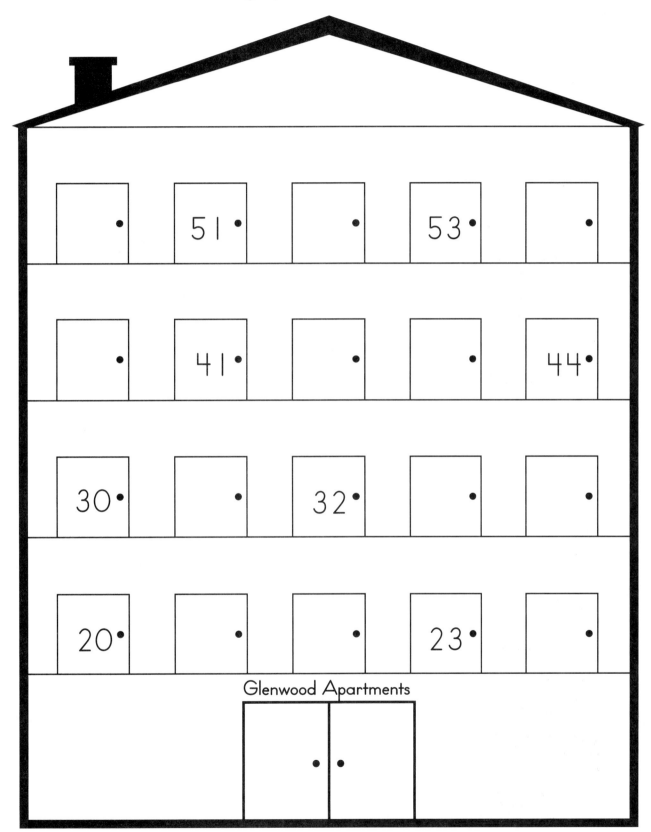

Glenwood Apartments

Ten, More or Less

Directions: Find **ten more** and **ten less** than the number given. The first one has been done for you.

1. 37  47 57

2. ____  82 ____

3. ____  36 ____

4. ____  79 ____

5. ____ 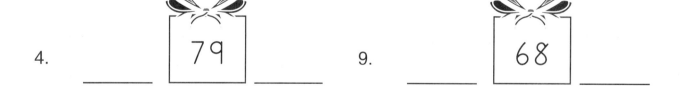 20 ____

6. ____  53 ____

7. ____  41 ____

8. ____ 74 ____

9. ____ 68 ____

10. ____  85 ____

Places Everyone

Directions: Label, with **ordinal** numbers, the place each person occupies in line. Then, answer the questions at the bottom of the page.

1. Matt _____
2. Sue _____
3. Mary _____
4. Daniel _____
5. Andrew _____
6. Max _____

first   second   third   fourth   fifth   sixth

7. Who is before Matt? _____

8. Who is after Max? _____

9. Who is at the end of the line? _____

Finish Line

Directions: Color the cars. Then, write the color of the car to show the place in which each will finish the race.

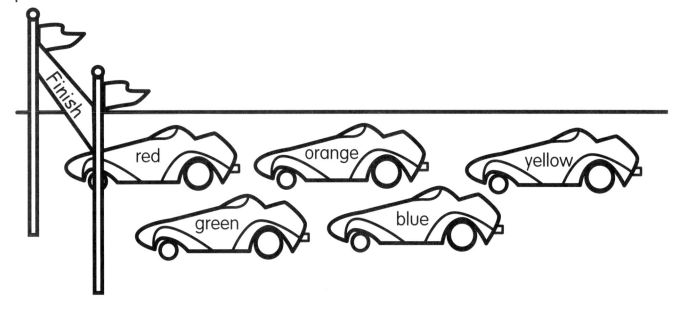

1. First _____

2. Third _____

3. Fifth _____

4. Second _____

5. Last _____

6. Fourth _____

7. What color is the car **before** the green car? _____

8. What color is the car **after** the blue car? _____

9. What color is the car **after** the red car? _____

10. What color is the car **before** the orange car? _____

Numbers Large and Small

Directions: Circle the **greater** number.

1. 19 13	2. 73 81	3. 24 21	4. 37 26	5. 62 78
6. 53 58	7. 73 81	8. 24 21	9. 37 26	10. 62 78

Directions: Circle the **lesser** number.

11. 17 21	12. 47 32	13. 58 51	14. 75 79	15. 80 91
16. 33 27	17. 66 56	18. 81 88	19. 37 43	20. 16 26

Greater Than, Less Than

Directions: Compare the numbers using **>**, **<**, and **=**. The first one has been done for you.

1. 43 $<$ 62

2. 73 ◯ 31

3. 57 ◯ 76

4. 67 ◯ 47

5. 39 ◯ 44

6. 58 ◯ 43

7. 39 ◯ 26

8. 73 ◯ 73

9. 42 ◯ 52

10. 28 ◯ 19

11. 83 ◯ 74

12. 18 ◯ 38

13. 19 ◯ 19

14. 93 ◯ 97

15. 48 ◯ 36

Counting by 10s

Directions: Count by **10s** to fill in the blank lines. Then, complete the dot-to-dot, counting by **10s**.

10, 20, _____ , _____ , 50,

60, _____ , _____ , _____ , 100

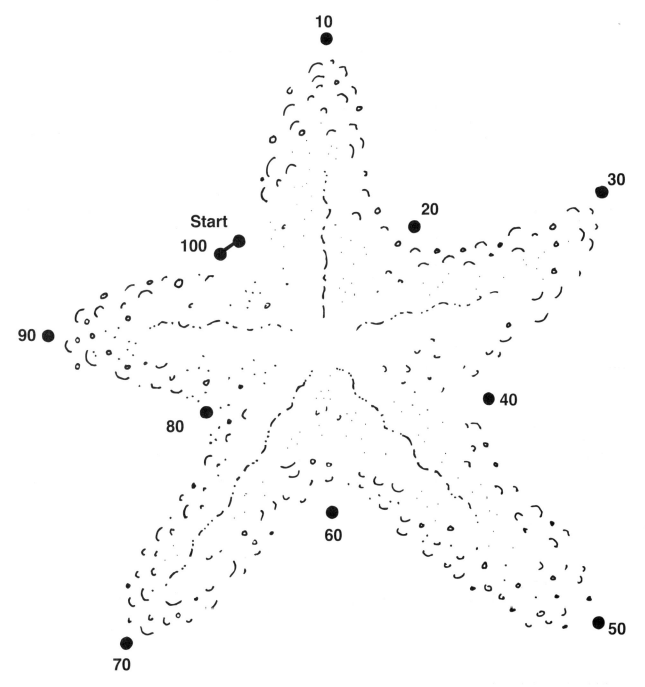

Counting by 5s

Directions: Help Max get home by counting by 5s.

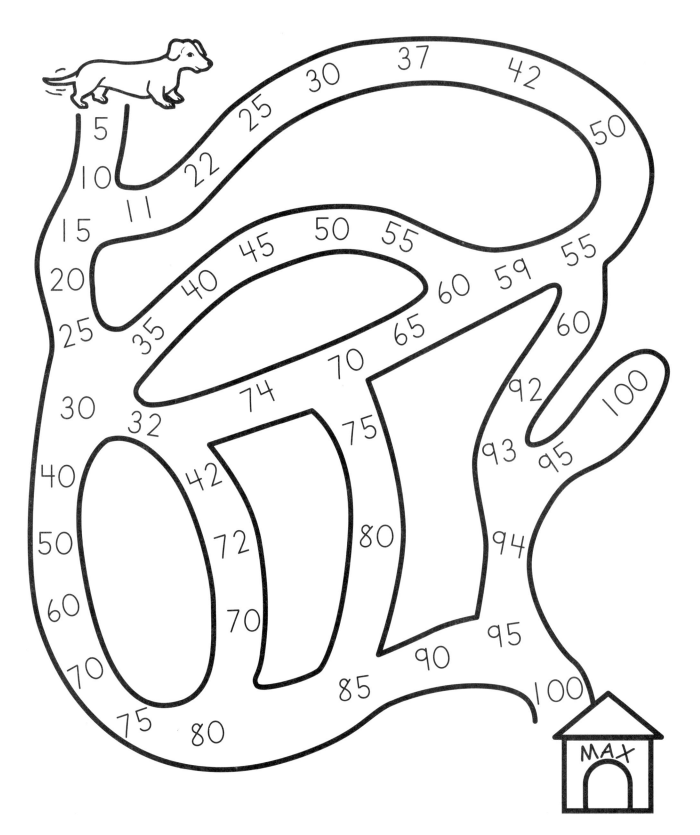

132   ©Teacher Created Resources, Inc.

Counting by 2s

Directions: Color the numbers you say when counting by **2s**.

1	2	3	4	5	6	7	8	9	10
11	12	13	14	15	16	17	18	19	20
21	22	23	24	25	26	27	28	29	30
31	32	33	34	35	36	37	38	39	40
41	42	43	44	45	46	47	48	49	50
51	52	53	54	55	56	57	58	59	60
61	62	63	64	65	66	67	68	69	70
71	72	73	74	75	76	77	78	79	80
81	82	83	84	85	86	87	88	89	90
91	92	93	94	95	96	97	98	99	100

What kind of pattern do you see? _____

_____

Counting Body Parts

Directions: Skip count in order to solve the problems. The first one has been done for you.

1. How many eyes on 7 boys?

2 + 2 + 2 + 2 + 2 + 2 + 2

_____14_____

2. How many **elbows** on 4 **men**?

_____

3. How many **mouths** on 7 **grandmas**?

_____

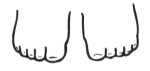

4. How many **toes** on 5 **babies**?

_____

5. How many **knees** on 5 **grandpas**?

_____

6. How many **feet** on 3 **brothers**?

_____

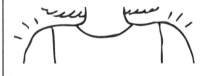

7. How many **shoulders** on 2 **teachers**?

_____

8. How many **ears** on 4 **fathers**?

_____

9. How many **noses** on 9 **women**?

_____

10. How many **fingers** on 6 **girls**?

_____

11. How many **faces** on 7 **people**?

_____

12. How many **ankles** on 4 **people**?

_____

Skip Counting Problem Solving

Directions: Solve the problems. Draw or write in the space to show your work.

1. Susan paints the fingernails of 4 friends. How many fingernails did she paint?

2. When Tim and his two brothers come home from school, his mom makes them take their shoes off at the door. How many shoes are by the door?

3. Karly's goal is to read 2 books every night. How many books will she need to read in 1 week?

4. There are 10 tennis balls in a box. Kim buys 7 boxes of tennis balls. How many tennis balls does Kim buy?

Odd or Even

Directions: Look at the number in each box. Decide if it is **odd** or **even**.
Circle the correct word.

1. 2 odd even	2. 13 odd even	3. 4 odd even	4. 8 odd even	5. 9 odd even	6. 20 odd even
7. 17 odd even	8. 12 odd even	9. 15 odd even	10. 16 odd even	11. 6 odd even	12. 1 odd even

Directions: Color the **even** numbers **yellow**. Color the **odd** numbers **blue**.
Find the mystery numbers.

2	90	38	46	88	12	92	44	68
92	3	22	23	66	17	87	1	4
56	15	98	11	36	45	16	91	24
58	57	39	75	6	27	59	73	54
8	72	50	29	62	78	100	69	10
40	48	26	47	14	32	52	37	48
18	96	70	96	86	38	20	42	80

The **odd** mystery number is _____.

The **even** mystery number is _____.

Show Addition

Directions: Write a **number sentence** to go with each picture.

1.

___ + ___ = ___

4.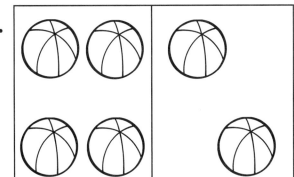

___ + ___ = ___

2.

___ + ___ = ___

5.

___ + ___ = ___

3.

___ + ___ = ___

6.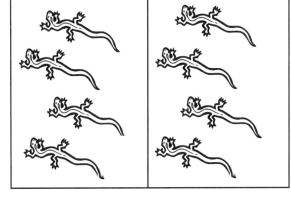

___ + ___ = ___

Ways to Make 6

Directions: Color the stars to match the **number sentence**. Use different colors for each group of stars in the sentence. The first one has been done for you.

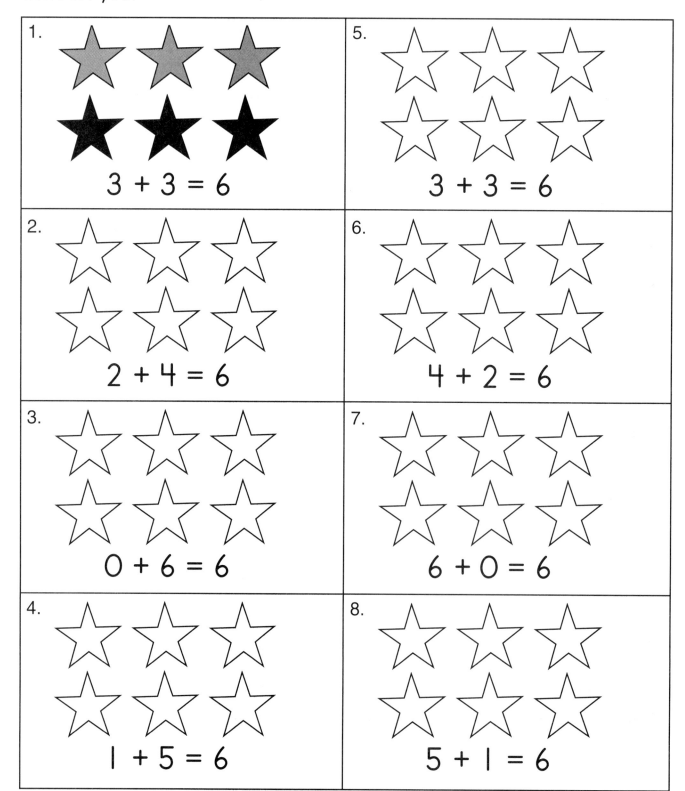

1. 3 + 3 = 6

2. 2 + 4 = 6

3. 0 + 6 = 6

4. 1 + 5 = 6

5. 3 + 3 = 6

6. 4 + 2 = 6

7. 6 + 0 = 6

8. 5 + 1 = 6

Addition Mystery Picture

Directions: Solve each **addition** problem. Then, color using the code below.

1-4 = Red 5-6 = Orange 7-8 = Yellow 9-10 = Blue

Ways to Equal a Sum

Directions: Circle the **addends** that equal the sum in the clouds. There may be more than one way to equal the sum.

1. **8**   2 + 2   5 + 4   3 + 5   7 + 1   6 + 2   4 + 3

2. **4**   2 + 2   3 + 2   4 + 0   5 + 1   3 + 1   0 + 4

3. **6**   6 + 0   2 + 5   4 + 2   3 + 3   5 + 1   6 + 2

4. **2**   2 + 0   3 + 1   4 + 1   1 + 1   0 + 2   1 + 2

5. **9**   4 + 6   3 + 6   1 + 8   1 + 9   8 + 2   9 + 0

6. **3**   3 + 1   2 + 0   3 + 0   2 + 1   0 + 3   1 + 2

7. **7**   6 + 1   2 + 5   3 + 5   6 + 3   4 + 3   7 + 0

8. **5**   2 + 2   5 + 0   3 + 2   1 + 4   4 + 2   3 + 2

Missing Addends

Directions: Find the missing **addends.** Use the letters to answer the question.

Why did the chicken cross the playground?

1. $3 + \boxed{} = 4$
   E

2. $3 + \boxed{} = 8$
   H

3. $\boxed{} + 5 = 9$
   R

4. $4 + \boxed{} = 7$
   O

5. $\boxed{} + 5 = 7$
   T

6. $\boxed{} + 0 = 10$
   D

7. $\boxed{} + 2 = 9$
   I

8. $8 + \boxed{} = 8$
   S

9. $1 + \boxed{} = 9$
   L

8. $3 + \boxed{} = 9$
   G

$\overline{2}\ \overline{3}$ $\overline{6}\ \overline{1}\ \overline{2}$ $\overline{2}\ \overline{3}$ $\overline{2}\ \overline{5}\ \overline{1}$

$\overline{3}\ \overline{2}\ \overline{5}\ \overline{1}\ \overline{4}$ $0\ 9\ 7\ 10\ 1$

Equal on Both Sides

Directions: Write the missing **addend** in order to make the equation equal on both sides of the equal sign. Cross off the numbers you use on the boat at the bottom of the page.

1. $2 + 3 = 3 + \boxed{}$

2. $4 + 1 = 1 + \boxed{}$

3. $3 + \boxed{} = 5 + 3$

4. $4 + 0 = \boxed{} + 4$

5. $6 + 2 = 2 + \boxed{}$

6. $\boxed{} + 3 = 3 + 7$

7. $2 + 5 = 5 + \boxed{}$

8. $\boxed{} + 5 = 5 + 1$

9. $2 + \boxed{} = 8 + 2$

10. $\boxed{} + 1 = 1 + 9$

Make Them Equal

Directions: Write a missing 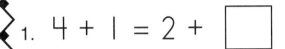 in order to make the equation equal on both sides of the equal sign.

1. $4 + 1 = 2 + \boxed{}$

2. $2 + 8 = 7 + \boxed{}$

3. $4 + \boxed{} = 6 + 1$

4. $\boxed{} + 0 = 2 + 2$

5. $3 + \boxed{} = 4 + 2$

6. $5 + \boxed{} = 8 + 1$

7. $6 + 2 = 4 + \boxed{}$

8. $8 + 0 = \boxed{} + 7$

9. $\boxed{} + 2 = 3 + 4$

10. $9 + \boxed{} = 4 + 5$

Challenge: $18 + 2 = 14 + \boxed{}$

Writing Number Sentences

Directions: Place a paperclip on the X. Then, place the tip of a pencil inside the paperclip. Use the paperclip as a spinner. Spin the paperclip around the pencil. The paperclip will act as the pointer.

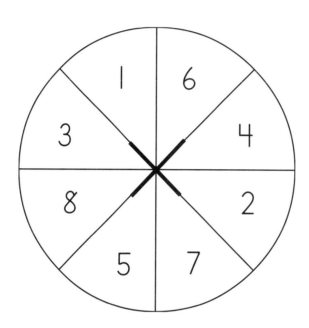

Spin the paperclip two times for each problem. Use the numbers that are spun as the **addends**. Solve the problem.

1. _____ + _____ = _____   6. _____ + _____ = _____

2. _____ + _____ = _____   7. _____ + _____ = _____

3. _____ + _____ = _____   8. _____ + _____ = _____

4. _____ + _____ = _____   9. _____ + _____ = _____

5. _____ + _____ = _____   10. _____ + _____ = _____

Addition Wheels

Directions: Add the number in the center circle to each number in the middle circle. Write each **sum** in the outer circle.

1.

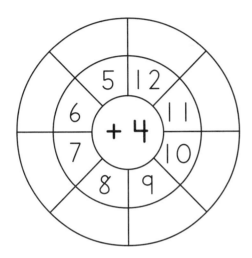

4.

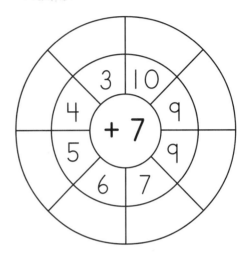

2.

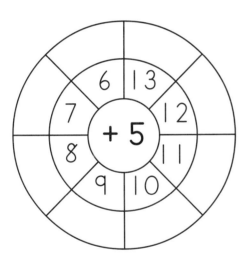

5.

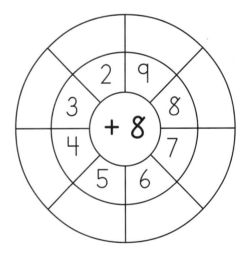

3.

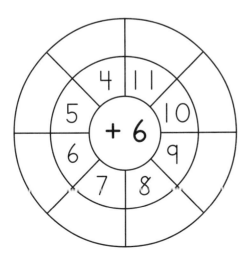

6.

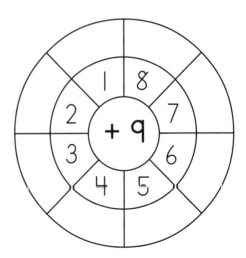

Addition Crossword

Directions: Solve the problems using **number names**. Write the **number names** in the crossword puzzle.

Across

1. 8 + 6 =
2. 10 + 7 =
3. 7 + 5 =
4. 9 + 9 =

Down

3. 14 + 6 =
5. 6 + 7 =
6. 9 + 6 =
7. 8 + 2 =

8. 5 + 6 =
9. 12 + 7 =
10. 8 + 8 =

Word Bank

ten
eleven
twelve
thirteen
fourteen
fifteen
sixteen
seventeen
eighteen
nineteen
twenty

Adding 3 Numbers

Directions: Solve each problem. Use the sums to figure out what to color the fish in the tank below.

1. $\begin{array}{r} 3 \\ 2 \\ +\ 5 \\ \hline \end{array}$ Green	2. $\begin{array}{r} 4 \\ 1 \\ +\ 3 \\ \hline \end{array}$ Blue	3. $\begin{array}{r} 5 \\ 5 \\ +\ 2 \\ \hline \end{array}$ Red
4. $\begin{array}{r} 6 \\ 1 \\ +\ 0 \\ \hline \end{array}$ Orange	5. $\begin{array}{r} 3 \\ 4 \\ +\ 4 \\ \hline \end{array}$ Yellow	6. $\begin{array}{r} 5 \\ 7 \\ +\ 1 \\ \hline \end{array}$ Purple
7. $\begin{array}{r} 4 \\ 3 \\ +\ 2 \\ \hline \end{array}$ Pink	8. $\begin{array}{r} 3 \\ 2 \\ +\ 1 \\ \hline \end{array}$ Brown	9. $\begin{array}{r} 6 \\ 5 \\ +\ 3 \\ \hline \end{array}$ Black

Addition Word Problems

Directions: Solve the **word problems** below. Show your work with a number sentence or a picture on the right.

1. Tom has 3 toy cars. He gets 2 more for his birthday. How many toy cars does Tom have now? _____	Show Your Work
2. Sarah and Michelle are playing together. Kim and her sister come to play with them. How many girls are playing? _____	Show Your Work
3. Micah has 8 trading cards. He buys 5 more. How many trading cards does Micah have in all? _____	Show Your Work
4. Ryanna checked out 2 books from the school library. She checked out some more books from the city library. She has 7 books in all. How many books did she check out from the city library? _____	Show Your Work

Show Subtraction

Directions: Write a **number sentence** to go with each picture.

1.

_____ – _____ = _____

4.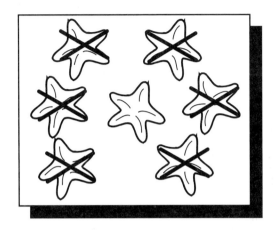

_____ – _____ = _____

2.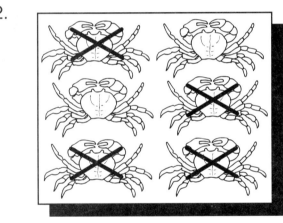

_____ – _____ = _____

5.

_____ – _____ = _____

3.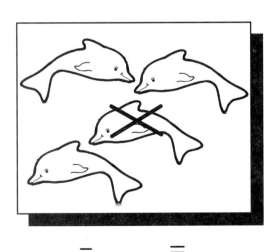

_____ – _____ = _____

6.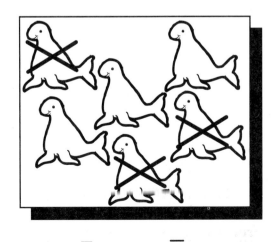

_____ – _____ = _____

Draw Subtraction

Directions: Draw a picture to illustrate each **number sentence**.

1.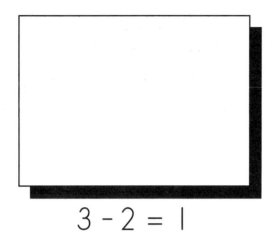

$$3 - 2 = 1$$

4.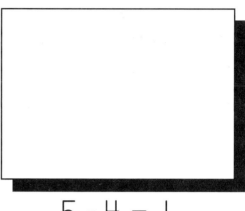

$$5 - 4 = 1$$

2.

$$4 - 2 = 2$$

5.

$$7 - 5 = 2$$

3.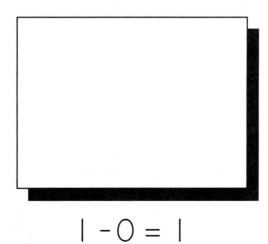

$$1 - 0 = 1$$

6.

$$3 - 1 = 2$$

Odd or Even?

Directions: Solve the **subtraction** problems below. Then, color the box using the key below.

Odd = Blue   Even = Red

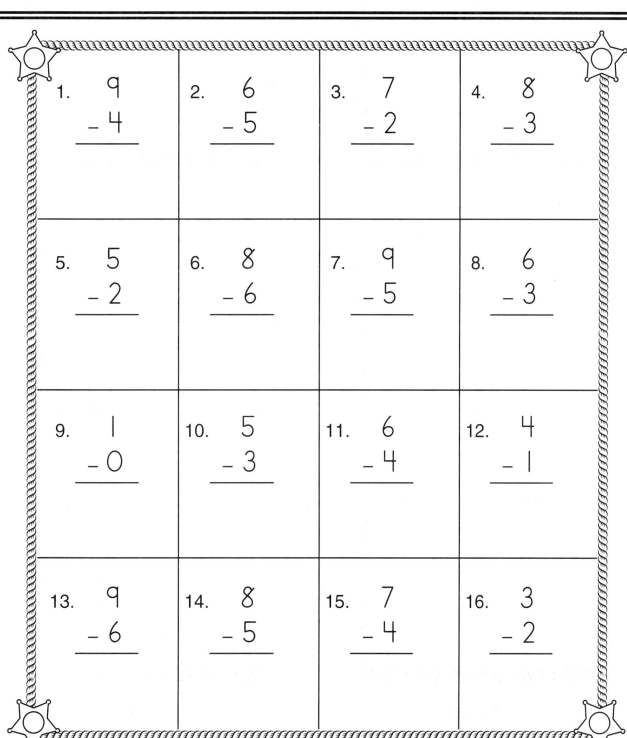

1.
  9
- 4

2.
  6
- 5

3.
  7
- 2

4.
  8
- 3

5.
  5
- 2

6.
  8
- 6

7.
  9
- 5

8.
  6
- 3

9.
  1
- 0

10.
  5
- 3

11.
  6
- 4

12.
  4
- 1

13.
  9
- 6

14.
  8
- 5

15.
  7
- 4

16.
  3
- 2

Subtraction Machines

Directions: Apply the rule at the top of each box to the numbers on the left. Write the differences in the boxes on the right.

1.

− 5	
7	
9	
5	
6	

2.

− 3	
4	
6	
5	
9	

3.

− 7	
8	
7	
9	
10	

4.

− 6	
6	
9	
8	
7	

5.

− 1	
9	
4	
2	
6	

6.

− 4	
5	
8	
4	
7	

7.

− 8	
8	
10	
9	
11	

8.

− 2	
3	
5	
7	
2	

9.

− 3	
4	
9	
5	
8	

What's Missing?

Directions: Write the missing numbers to complete the **number sentence**. Color the numbers in the balloons as you use them.

1. 7 − ☐ = 5

2. 4 − ☐ = 1

3. ☐ − 4 = 4

4. 8 − ☐ = 5

5. 9 − ☐ = 6

6. 6 − ☐ = 4

7. ☐ − 2 = 3

8. ☐ − 1 = 2

9. 7 − ☐ = 3

10. 8 − ☐ = 6

Subtraction Wheels

Directions: Write a number in the middle circle so that when it is **subtracted** from the number in the outer circle, the difference is the number in the center

1.

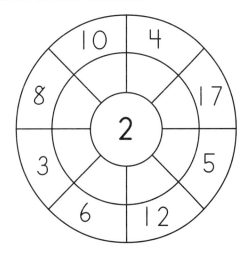

2.

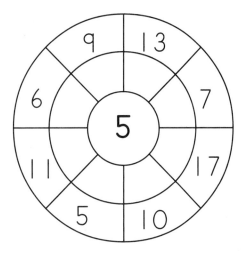

3.

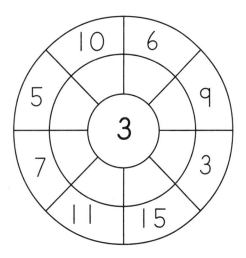

4.

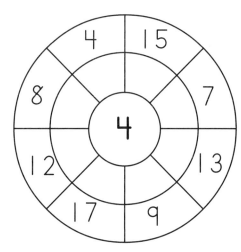

5.

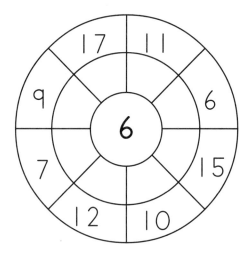

6.

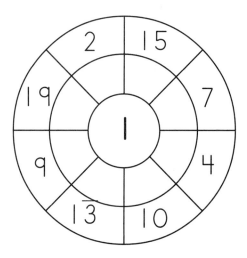

Subtraction Riddle

Directions: Solve each problem. Then, match each solution to the numbers at the bottom of the page. Write the corresponding letter in each blank to solve the riddle.

Why are seagulls called seagulls?

1. $\begin{array}{r} 9 \\ -4 \\ \hline \end{array}$ (R)

2. $\begin{array}{r} 14 \\ -5 \\ \hline \end{array}$ (G)

3. $\begin{array}{r} 19 \\ -7 \\ \hline \end{array}$ (Y)

4. $\begin{array}{r} 12 \\ -5 \\ \hline \end{array}$ (T)

5. $\begin{array}{r} 14 \\ -3 \\ \hline \end{array}$ (A)

6. $\begin{array}{r} 16 \\ -6 \\ \hline \end{array}$ (S)

7. $\begin{array}{r} 19 \\ -6 \\ \hline \end{array}$ (L)

8. $\begin{array}{r} 17 \\ -8 \\ \hline \end{array}$ (G)

9. $\begin{array}{r} 15 \\ -7 \\ \hline \end{array}$ (B)

10. $\begin{array}{r} 14 \\ -5 \\ \hline \end{array}$ (G)

11. $\begin{array}{r} 13 \\ -7 \\ \hline \end{array}$ (E)

12. $\begin{array}{r} 18 \\ -6 \\ \hline \end{array}$ (Y)

If they lived by the _____ _____ _____ , they would be
         8   11   12

called _____ _____ _____ _____ _____ _____ .
        8   11   9   13   6   10

Subtraction Word Problems

Directions: Solve the **word problems** below. Show your work with a number sentence or a picture on the right.

1. Tyler shoots 7 baskets. He misses 3 times. How many baskets did he make? _____	Show Your Work
2. Six children are playing hockey. Two children have to go home. How many children are left? _____	Show Your Work
3. There are five cookies on a plate. Mandi comes home from school and eats some. Now there are only two cookies on the plate. How many cookies did Mandi eat? _____	Show Your Work
4. Bernice's homework packet has 8 pages in it. She has completed 6 pages. How many more pages of homework does Bernice have to do? _____	Show Your Work

How Many?

Directions: Solve each problem. Write a number sentence to show your work.

1.  There are **7** cookies in all. How many are in the bag?

2.  There are **6** kittens in all. How many are in the box?

3.  There are **2** pencils in all. How many are in the box?

4. 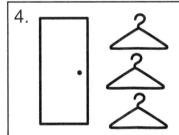 There are **20** hangers in all. How many are in the closet?

5.  There are **5** people in the family. How many are in the house?

Addition and Subtraction Machines

Directions: Apply the rule at the top of each box to the numbers on the left. Write the answers in the boxes on the right.

1.

− 4	
12	
8	
20	
15	

2.

+ 6	
9	
12	
7	
2	

3.

− 8	
17	
11	
20	
15	

4.

+ 3	
14	
9	
17	
4	

5.

+ 5	
14	
3	
12	
9	

6.

− 5	
15	
9	
18	
6	

7.

− 6	
19	
13	
9	
6	

8.

+ 1	
19	
15	
3	
9	

9.

− 4	
8	
17	
5	
13	

Addition and Subtraction Puzzle

Directions: Write the **missing numbers** to complete the number sentences.

$5 + 2 =$ [1.]

$- \ 3$

[2.] $+ \ 2 =$ [3.]

$+ \ 10$

$9 \ + $ [5.] $=$ [4.]

$- \ 5$

[6.] $-$ [7.] $= 3$

$+ \ 7$ $+ \ 9$

[8.] $+ \ 4 =$ [10.] $+$ [11.] $= 20$

$-$ [9.] $- \ 10$

8 [12.] $+ \ 3 =$ [13.]

$- \ 5$

$12 \ +$ [14.] $=$ [15.]

$+ \ 5$

[16.]

Farm Word Problems

Directions: Solve the **word problems** below. Show your work with a number sentence or a picture on the right.

1. There are 4 pigs on the farm. Eight baby pigs are born. Now how many pigs are on the farm?	Show Your Work
2. There are 6 sheep in the barn. There are 7 sheep in the field. How many sheep are there altogether?	Show Your Work
3. There are 7 kittens on the farm. The farmer keeps one for each of his three children. He gives the rest away to his children's friends. How many kittens does he give away?	Show Your Work
4. There are 5 cows being milked. Seven cows are waiting to be milked. Six cows have already been milked. How many cows are on the farm in all?	Show Your Work

Farm Word Problems *(cont.)*

Directions: Solve the word problems below. Show your work with a number sentence or a picture on the right.

5. There are eight goats on the farm. Six are sleeping. How many goats are awake?	Show Your Work
6. The farmer does not work on Sunday. The farmer could not plow his field on Tuesday because it rained. How many days was the farmer able to plow his field this week?	Show Your Work
7. The farmer has to milk the cows in the morning and in the evening. How many times does he have to milk the cows in one week?	Show Your Work
8. There are 9 ducks in the pond. Six ducks go into the barn. How many ducks are left in the pond?	Show Your Work

Missing Numbers

Directions: Fill in the missing numbers to complete the number sentences for each **fact family**.

1. $4 + 3 = \underline{\hspace{1cm}}$

   $\underline{\hspace{1cm}} + 4 = 7$

   $7 - 3 = \underline{\hspace{1cm}}$

   $7 - \underline{\hspace{1cm}} = 3$

4. $5 + \underline{\hspace{1cm}} = 8$

   $3 + \underline{\hspace{1cm}} = 8$

   $8 - 5 = \underline{\hspace{1cm}}$

   $8 - \underline{\hspace{1cm}} = 5$

7. $5 + \underline{\hspace{1cm}} = 7$

   $\underline{\hspace{1cm}} + 5 = 7$

   $7 - \underline{\hspace{1cm}} = 5$

   $7 - \underline{\hspace{1cm}} = 2$

2. $2 + 3 = \underline{\hspace{1cm}}$

   $3 + 2 = \underline{\hspace{1cm}}$

   $5 - \underline{\hspace{1cm}} = 3$

   $\underline{\hspace{1cm}} - 3 = 2$

5. $\underline{\hspace{1cm}} + 7 = 9$

   $\underline{\hspace{1cm}} + 2 = 9$

   $9 - 2 = \underline{\hspace{1cm}}$

   $9 - \underline{\hspace{1cm}} = 2$

8. $4 + \underline{\hspace{1cm}} = 9$

   $5 + \underline{\hspace{1cm}} = 9$

   $9 - 4 = \underline{\hspace{1cm}}$

   $\underline{\hspace{1cm}} - 5 = 4$

3. $4 + 1 = \underline{\hspace{1cm}}$

   $\underline{\hspace{1cm}} + 4 = 5$

   $5 - 1 = \underline{\hspace{1cm}}$

   $5 - \underline{\hspace{1cm}} = 1$

6. $4 + 2 = \underline{\hspace{1cm}}$

   $2 + \underline{\hspace{1cm}} = 6$

   $6 - \underline{\hspace{1cm}} = 4$

   $\underline{\hspace{1cm}} - 4 = 2$

9. $5 + 1 = \underline{\hspace{1cm}}$

   $\underline{\hspace{1cm}} + 5 = 6$

   $6 - \underline{\hspace{1cm}} = 5$

   $\underline{\hspace{1cm}} - 5 = 1$

Writing Fact Families

Directions: Use the numbers in each cloud to write a **fact family**. The first one has been done for you.

1. { 2, 3, 5 }

$2 + 3 = 5$

$3 + 2 = 5$

$5 - 3 = 2$

$5 - 2 = 3$

2. { 4, 5, 9 }

_____

_____

_____

_____

3. { 1, 2, 3 }

_____

_____

_____

_____

4. { 7, 2, 9 }

_____

_____

_____

_____

5. { 3, 5, 8 }

_____

_____

_____

_____

6. { 1, 8, 9 }

_____

_____

_____

_____

7. { 6, 4, 2 }

_____

_____

_____

_____

8. { 3, 4, 7 }

_____

_____

_____

_____

9. { 6, 3, 9 }

_____

_____

_____

_____

Coin Purses

Directions: Count the coins in each purse. Write the total amount of money on the line. The first one has been done for you.

1.

_____

2.

_____

3.

_____

4.

_____

5.

_____

6.

_____

7.

_____

8.

_____

Toy Store

Directions: Use the prices for the toys to help you answer the questions.

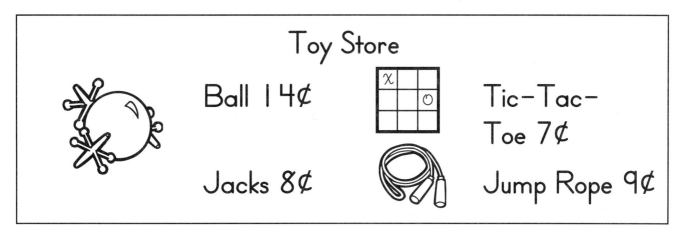

Toy Store

Ball 14¢

Jacks 8¢

Tic-Tac-Toe 7¢

Jump Rope 9¢

1. You want to buy a ball and jacks. What is the total cost? _____

2. You buy a jump rope for your sister and a ball for your brother. You buy jacks for yourself. What is the total cost? _____

3. You have a dime and a nickel. What two items can you buy? _____

4. You buy a jump rope and pay with a dime. How much is your change? _____

5. You have a dime. What items can you buy? (There are different possibilities.) _____

6. You only have a nickel. You want to buy a Tic-Tac-Toe board. How much money are you missing?

_____

Pay For It

Directions: Color in the coins that could be used to pay for each item. (There may be more than one combination of coins that will work.)

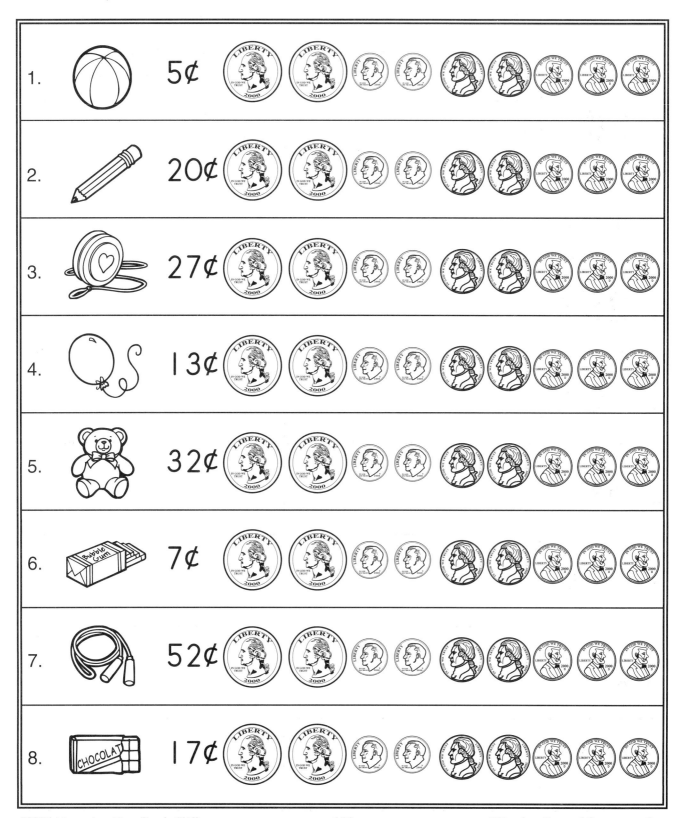

Two Different Methods

Directions: Show two different coin combinations that equal the amount shown. The first one has been done for you.

	Method 1	Method 2
1. 5¢		
2. 11¢		
3. 25¢		
4. 50¢		
5. 6¢		
6. 15¢		
7. 21¢		
8. 40¢		

Months of the Year

Directions: Read the poem below. Then, write the months in order at the bottom of the page. Determine how many days are in each **month**.

> Thirty days hath September
> April, June, and November.
> All the rest have thirty-one
> Excepting February alone,
> And that has twenty-eight days clear
> And twenty-nine each leap year.

December	June	February	August	October	May
November	April	January	March	September	July

1. January   31 days   7. _____ _____ days

2. _____ _____ days   8. _____ _____ days

3. _____ _____ days   9. _____ _____ days

4. _____ _____ days   10. _____ _____ days

5. _____ _____ days   11. _____ _____ days

6. _____ _____ days   12. _____ _____ days

Reading a Calendar

Directions: Use the **calendar** below to answer the questions at the bottom of the page.

February

SUNDAY	MONDAY	TUESDAY	WEDNESDAY	THURSDAY	FRIDAY	SATURDAY
		1	2	3	4	5
6	7	8	9	10	11	12
13	14 ♥ Valentine's Day	15	16	17	18	19
20	21	22	23	24	25	26
27	28					

1. What month is it? _____

2. How many days are in this month? _____

3. On what day of the week will Valentine's Day fall?

   _____

4. How many Saturdays are in this month? _____

5. On what day of the week will March 1st fall?

   _____

About How Long?

Directions: Read the list of activities below. Decide if each activity would take **seconds, minutes,** or **hours** to complete. Circle the correct response.

1. Go on a hike	seconds minutes hours
2. Write your name	seconds minutes hours
3. Eat breakfast	seconds minutes hours
4. Watch a movie	seconds minutes hours
5. Do one jumping jack	seconds minutes hours
6. Go on a long drive	seconds minutes hours
7. Write a letter to Grandma	seconds minutes hours
8. Count to 10	seconds minutes hours
9. Sing a song	seconds minutes hours
10. Brush your teeth	seconds minutes hours

What Time Is It?

Directions: Read the sentences below. Write the time shown on the clock in **digital time**. Then, circle either **A.M.** or **P.M.**

1. I get up at  _____ : **A.M.**

2. I eat breakfast at  _____ : **A.M.**

3. School starts at _____ : **A.M.**

4. Lunch is at _____ : **P.M.**

5. School ends at  _____ : **P.M.**

6. I practice piano at  _____ : **P.M.**

7. Dinner is served at  _____ : **P.M.**

8. I go to bed at 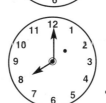 _____ : **P.M.**

Telling Time

Directions: Read the **digital time** shown below each clock. Then, draw an hour hand and a minute hand on the clock to show the same time.

1.
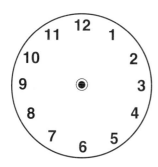

3:00

2.
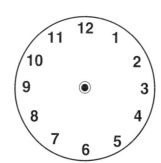

7:00

3.
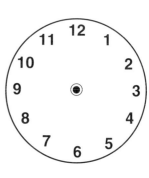

1:00

4.
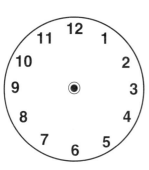

10:00

5.
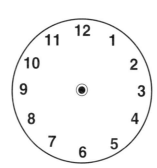

6:00

6.
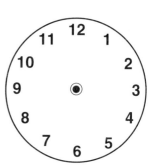

4:00

7.
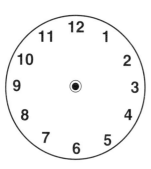

11:00

8.
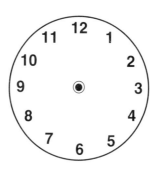

12:00

9.
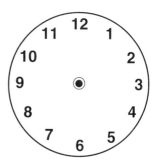

2:00

10. What time do you go to bed? _____

How Much Time?

Directions: The clocks below show the starting and ending times for each subject. Write the length of each class by calculating the **elapsed time**. The first one has been done for you.

Subject	Starts	Ends	Length of Class
1. Spelling	(clock)	(clock)	half an hour
2. Reading	(clock)	(clock)	
3. Music	(clock)	(clock)	
4. Math	(clock)	(clock)	
5. Science	(clock)	(clock)	
6. P.E.	(clock)	(clock)	

Inch, Foot, or Yard?

Directions: Complete the statements below by circling the correct **measurements.**

1. A penny measures about . . .   an inch   a foot   a yard

2. Your father's shoe measures
   about . . .   an inch   a foot   a yard

3. A dinner plate measures
   about . . .   an inch   a foot   a yard

4. A book measures about . . .   an inch   a foot   a yard

5. An eraser measures about. . .   an inch   a foot   a yard

6. A small table measures
   about. . .   an inch   a foot   a yard

7. A nail measures about. . .   an inch   a foot   a yard

8. A child's bicycle measures
   about. . .   an inch   a foot   a yard

9. A piece of candy measures
   about. . .   an inch   a foot   a yard

10. A hammer measures about. . .   an inch   a foot   a yard

Draw a picture of something that measures . . .

about one inch	about one foot	about one yard

Using a Ruler

Directions: Measure the objects below, using a ruler. Write the measurement of each object in inches on the appropriate lines.

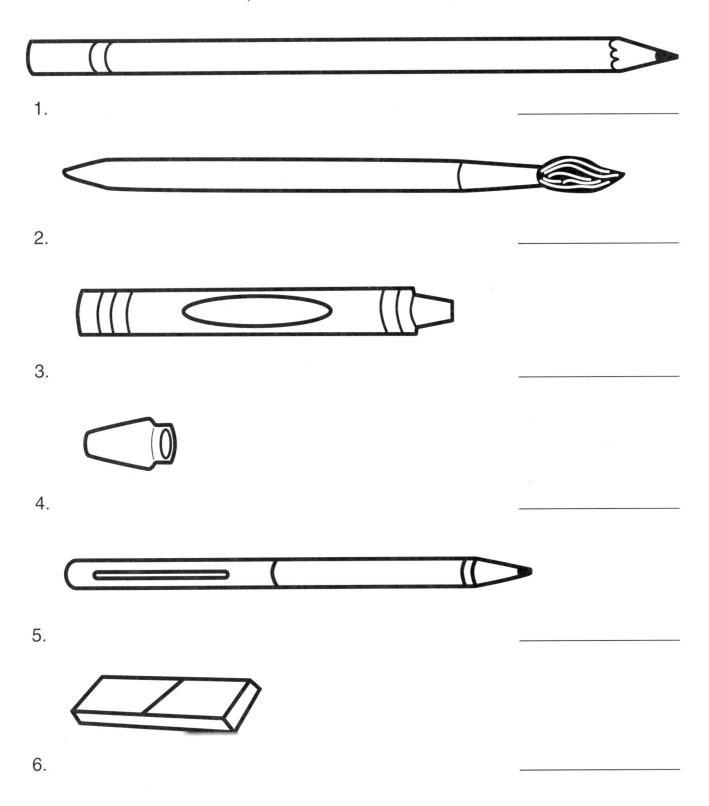

1. _____

2. _____

3. _____

4. _____

5. _____

6. _____

Leafy Measurement

Directions: Measure the following leaves in centimeters.

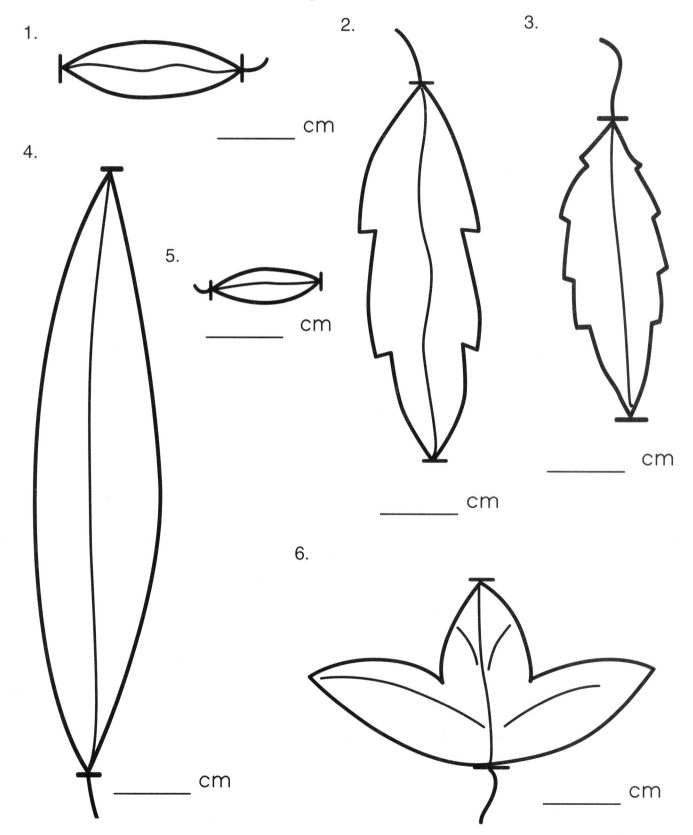

1.

_____ cm

2.

_____ cm

3.

_____ cm

4.

_____ cm

5.

_____ cm

6.

_____ cm

A Pound, More or Less

Directions: Look at the object in each box. Decide if the real object would weight **more than one pound** or **less than one pound**.

1. **a paperclip**  more than one pound less than one pound	2. **a cat** more than one pound less than one pound	3. **a chair** more than one pound less than one pound
4. **a door** more than one pound less than one pound	5. **an eraser**  more than one pound less than one pound	6. **a person** more than one pound less than one pound
7. **a piece of paper**  more than one pound less than one pound	8. **a computer**  more than one pound less than one pound	9. **a pencil**  more than one pound less than one pound
10. **a spoon**  more than one pound less than one pound	11. **a truck**  more than one pound less than one pound	12. **a pig** more than one pound less than one pound

Heavy and Light

Directions: Draw a seesaw on the balancing point to show which object is **heavier** and which object is **lighter**.

Example:

1.

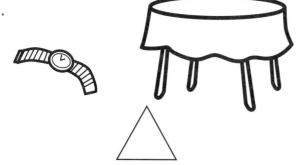

4.

2.

5.

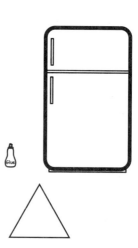

3.

6.

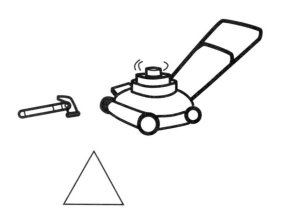

Measuring Tools

Directions: Use the words on the right to complete each riddle.

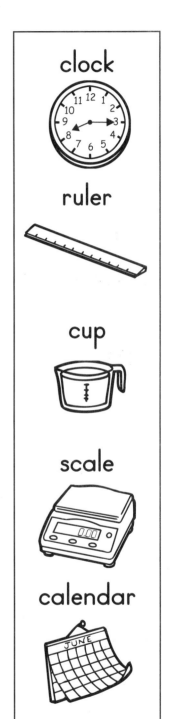

1. I am used to show the date.

   What am I? I am a _____.

2. I am used to show how much something weighs.

   What am I? I am a _____.

3. I am used to check length and height.

   What am I? I am a _____.

4. I am used to tell time.

   What am I? I am a _____.

5. I am used to show volume.

   What am I? I am a _____.

clock

ruler

cup

scale

calendar

Create a Clown

Directions: Follow the directions in order to draw a picture of a clown.

1. Draw a **circle** for the **head.**

2. Draw an **oval** below the circle for the **body.**

3. Draw a **triangle** above the head for the **hat.**

4. Draw two vertical **rectangles** below the oval for the **legs.**

5. Draw two horizontal **rectangles**, one on the left and one on the right side of the oval, for the **arms.**

6. Draw **hands, shoes,** and a **face.** Add other details to the clown picture, such as balloons.

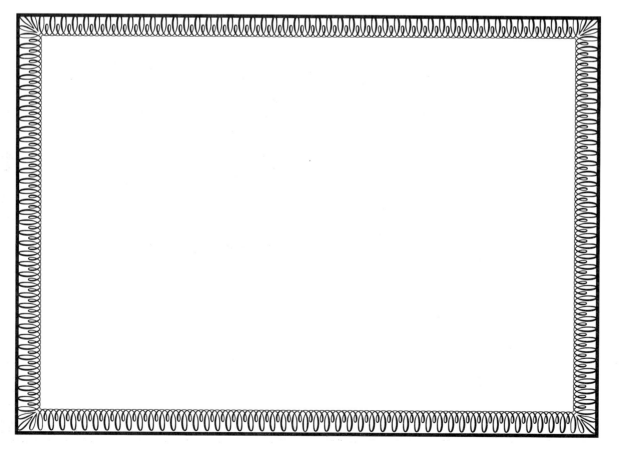

Create a Picture

Directions: Follow the directions to complete the picture.

1. Draw a **sun** in the **top left corner.**

2. Draw a **duck** in the **pond.**

3. Draw a **person** on the **bench.**

4. Draw a **dog** beside the **person.**

5. Draw a **trashcan** next to the **bench.**

Shape Riddles

Directions: Answer each riddle with the name or names of the **shapes** below. Some of the riddles may have more than one answer.

circle   square   triangle   rectangle   pentagon   hexagon

1. I am round all the way around. What am I? _____

2. I have 4 sides. What am I? _____

3. I have 3 corners. What am I? _____

4. I have 6 sides. What am I? _____

5. I have equal sides. What am I? _____

6. I have 5 sides and corners. What am I?_____

7. I have 4 corners. What am I? _____

8. I have 2 long sides and 2 short sides. What am I?

_____

Identifying Solids

Directions: Match the picture of the solid to its name by drawing a line. Then, complete the sentences below.

1.   rectangular prism

2. 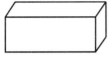   cylinder

3.   cone

4.   cube

5.   pyramid

6.   sphere

7. A **shoebox** is the shape of _____.

8. An **ice cream cone** is the shape of _____.

9. A **ball** is the shape of _____.

10. A **soup can** is the shape of _____.

Lines of Symmetry

Directions: Draw a **line of symmetry** on the figures below. Draw an **X** across the figure if a **line of symmetry** cannot be drawn. Some figures may have many more than **one line of symmetry**. The first one has been done for you.

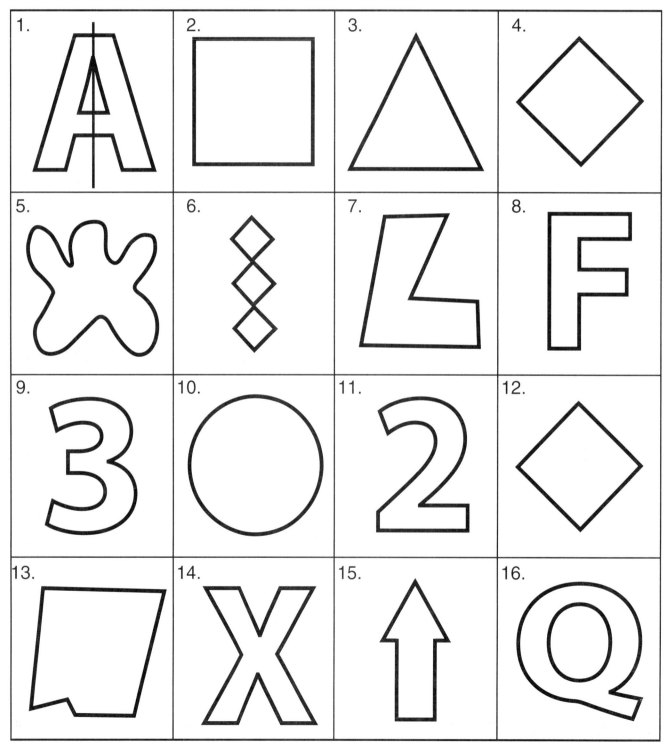

Draw Equal Parts

Directions: Draw a line to show two **equal parts**.

1.   2.   3.

Directions: Draw lines to show three **equal parts**.

4.   5.   6.

Directions: Draw lines to show four **equal parts**.

7.   8.   9.

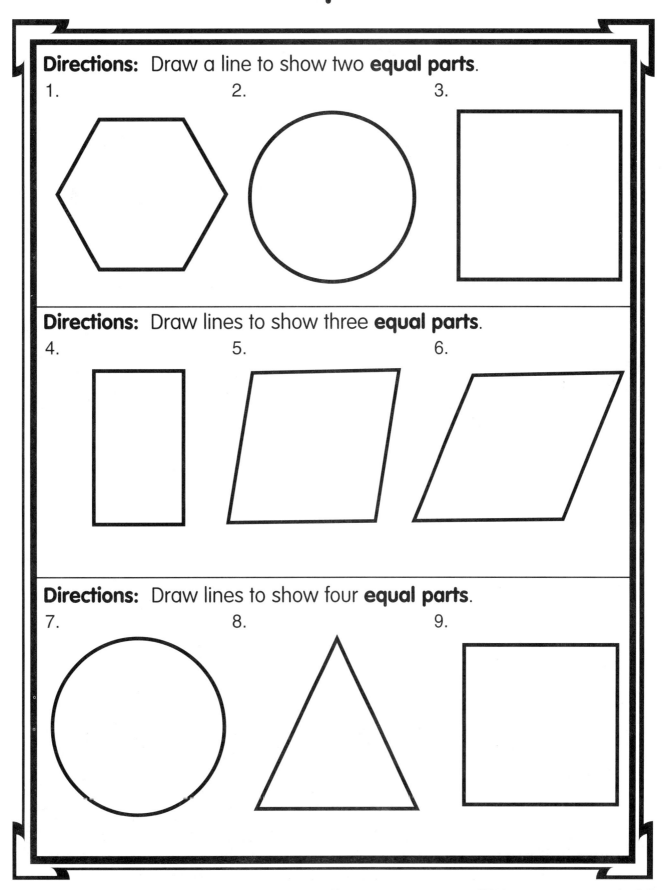

Name the Fraction

Directions: Write a **fraction** for each picture. The first one has been done for you.

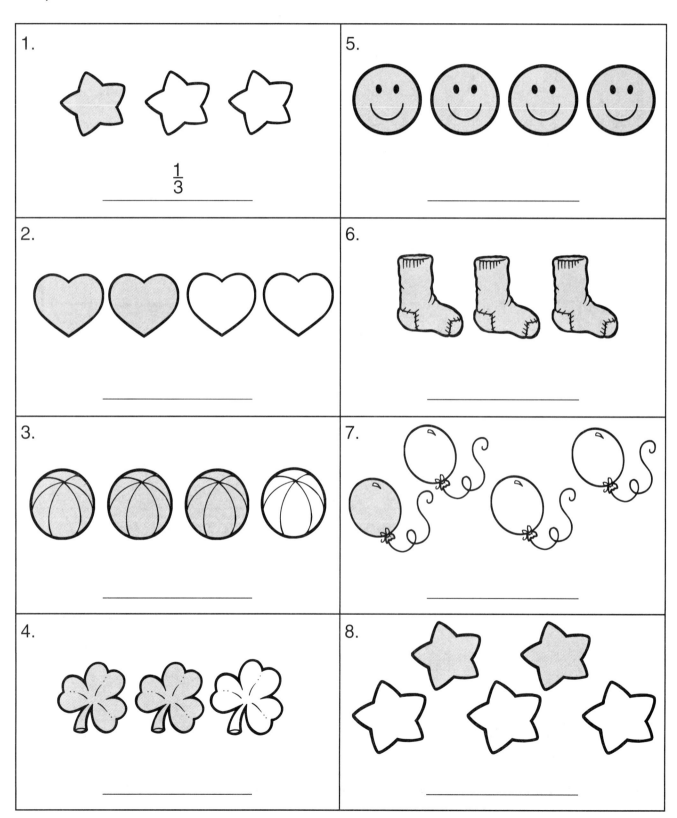

1.

$\frac{1}{3}$

_____

2.

_____

3.

_____

4.

_____

5.

_____

6.

_____

7.

_____

8.

_____

Coloring Fractions

Directions: Color the correct part of each shape to match the **fraction**. The first one has been done for you.

1.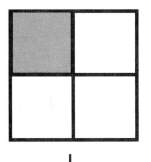

$\dfrac{1}{4}$

2.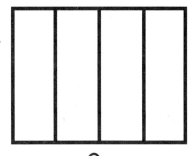

$\dfrac{2}{4}$

3.

$\dfrac{1}{3}$

4.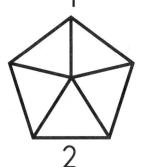

$\dfrac{2}{5}$

5.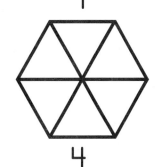

$\dfrac{4}{6}$

6.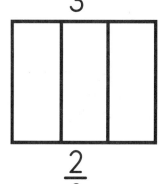

$\dfrac{2}{3}$

7.

$\dfrac{1}{2}$

8.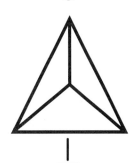

$\dfrac{1}{3}$

9.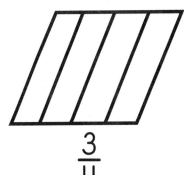

$\dfrac{3}{4}$

10.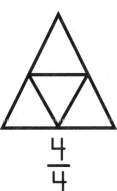

$\dfrac{4}{4}$

11.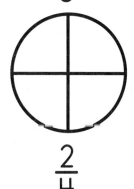

$\dfrac{2}{4}$

12.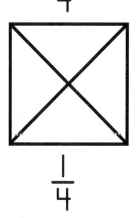

$\dfrac{1}{4}$

Sort by Attribute

Directions: Sort the objects by coloring those that match the category in each square.

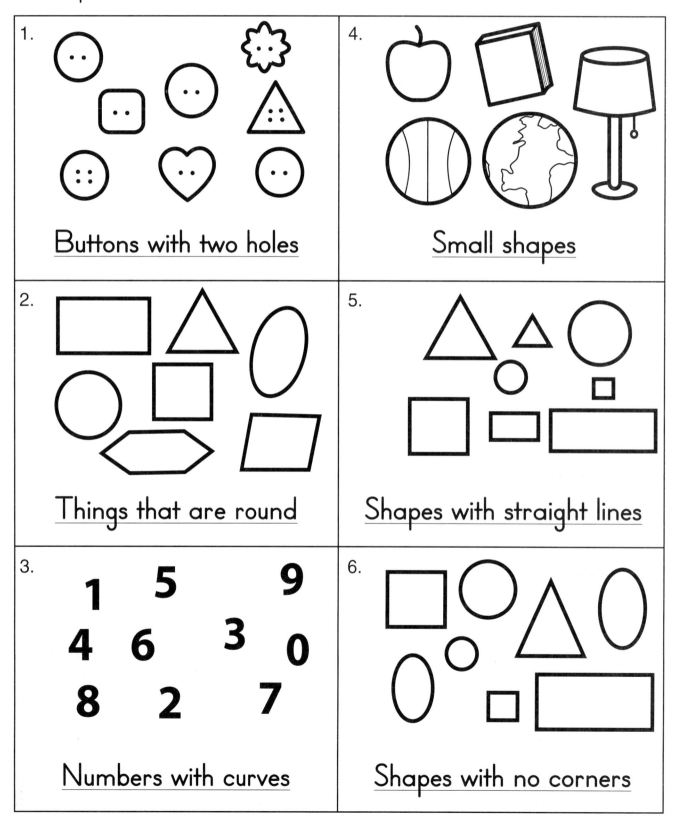

1. Buttons with two holes

4. Small shapes

2. Things that are round

5. Shapes with straight lines

3. Numbers with curves

6. Shapes with no corners

Create a Pattern

Directions: Color the shapes below to create the **pattern** shown. The first one has been partially done for you.

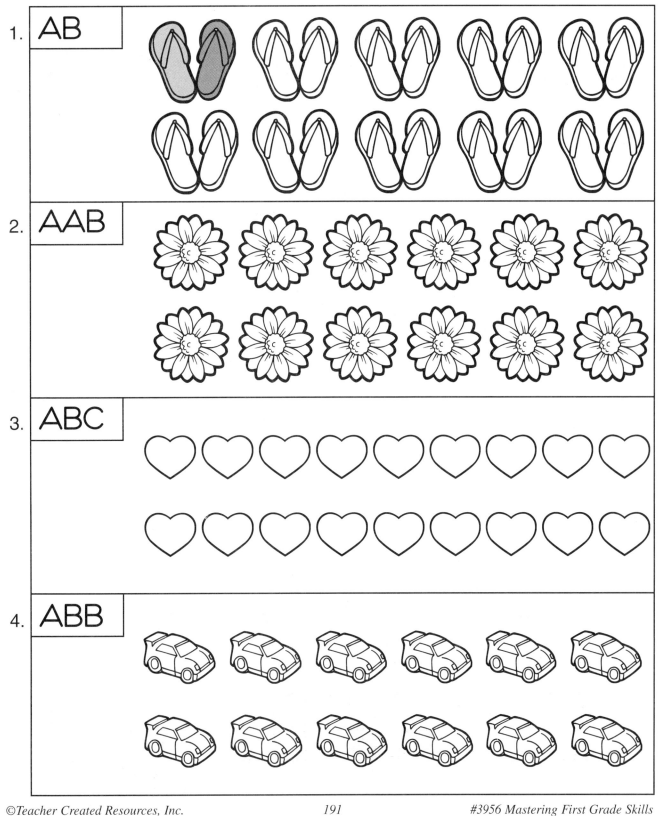

Number Patterns

Directions: Extend the number patterns below, by adding the correct numbers.

1. 1, 2, 3, 4, _____, _____, _____

2. 1, 2, 4, 7, _____, _____, _____

3. 2, 6, 10, 14, _____, _____, _____

4. 28, 26, 24, 22, _____, _____, _____

5. 1, 2, 4, 8, 16, _____, _____, _____

6. 90, 80, 70, 60, _____, _____, _____

7. 37, 36, 35, 34, _____, _____, _____

8. 75, 70, 65, 60, _____, _____, _____

Count the Animals

Directions: Count the animals in the picture. Use **tally marks** below to show how many animals of each kind live on the farm.

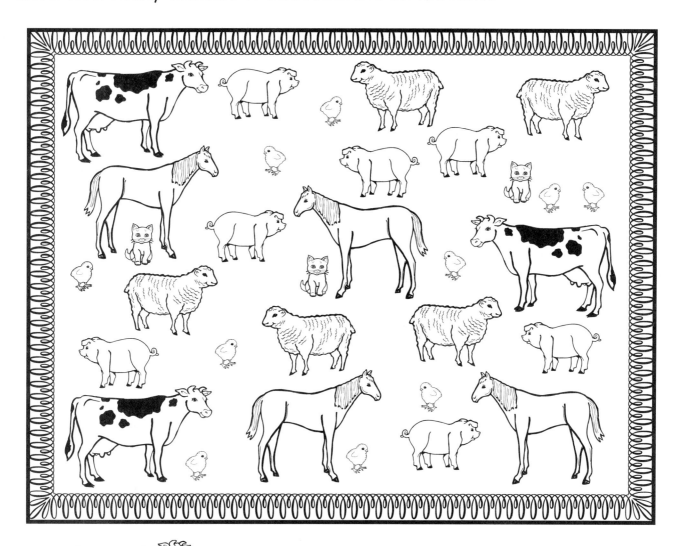

1. _____

2. _____

3. _____

4. _____

5. _____

6. _____

Graphing Books

Directions: Use the information below to create a **bar graph**. Then, answer the questions at the bottom of the page.

6 books — Mark
7 books — Maria
3 books — Julio
5 books — Kim
4 books — Stephan
6 books — Marissa

1. Which child read the most books? _____
2. How many more books did Maria read than Kim? _____
3. Who read the fewest books? _____
4. Which students read the same number of books?

_____

Graph a Fish Bowl

Directions: Tally the objects in the fish bowl. Then, create a **bar graph** of the tallied information.

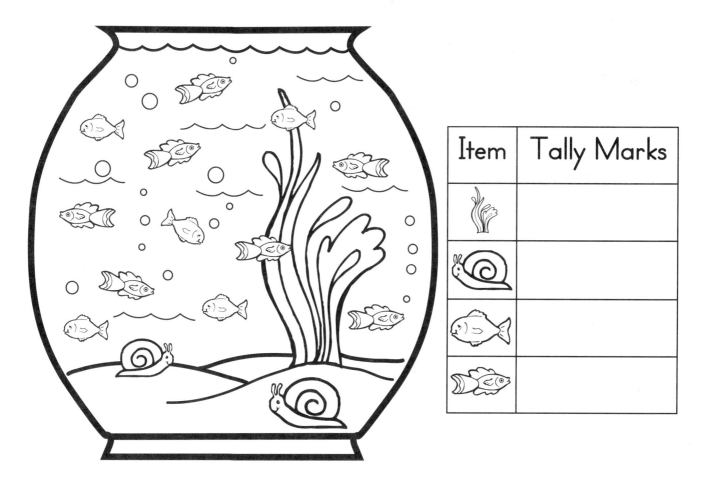

Item	Tally Marks
🌿	
🐌	
🐟	
🐟	

Item	1	2	3	4	5	6	7	8
🌿								
🐌								
🐟								
🐟								

Using a Bar Graph

Directions: Look at the bar **graph** below. Each square represents one child. Then, answer the questions about the bar **graph**.

Favorite Sport

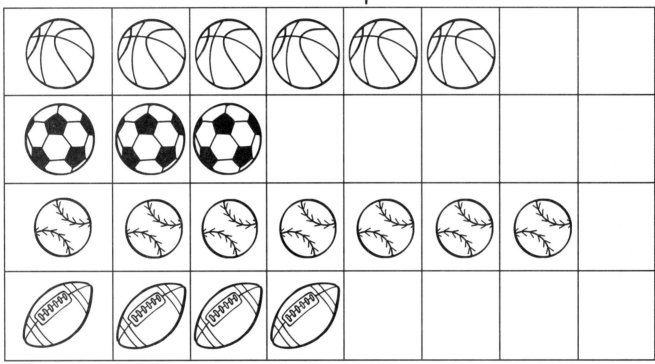

1. Which sport was the favorite sport?

 basketball   baseball

 soccer   football

2. How many children liked football?_____

3. How many more children liked soccer than basketball?_____

4. How many children liked soccer and football?

_____

5. What is your favorite sport?_____

196

Problem Solving

Directions: Solve the problems below. Show your work in the space provided.

1. Three children had a race at recess. Tony came in last. Sarah came in after Mark. Who came in first? Who came in second? Who came in third?

2. Jose invited five children to his birthday party. He wants to give each child two balloons, including himself. How many balloons does Jose need to buy?

3. Maurice is going to buy lunch at school on Tuesday. He will bring his lunch on all other school days. How many days must he pack his lunch?

4. Brenda gets five cents for each bottle she recycles. How much money will she earn if she recycles 10 bottles?

More Problem Solving

Directions: Solve the problems below. Show your work in the space provided.

1. Marie has eight pieces of candy. She wants to share them equally with her friend Joanne. How many pieces of candy will each girl get?

2. Sean wants to give three friends each five sticks of gum. Each pack of gum has five sticks of gum. How many packs of gum does Sean have to buy?

3. Mary is three years older than her brother Tim. Tim is four years old. How old is Mary?

4. It takes Emily 10 minutes to walk to school and 10 minutes to walk home from school. How many minutes does Emily spend walking to and from school each week?

What Would You Do?

Directions: Read the activities in the box below. Sort them into things you would do on a **sunny day** and things you would do on a **rainy day**.

 have a picnic   wear shorts

 use an umbrella   go to the park

 stomp in puddles   climb a tree

 wear rain boots   float leaves in the water

Sunny Day 	Rainy Day
1.	1.
2.	2.
3.	3.
4.	4.

Dress for the Weather

Directions: Use the words from the Word Bank to complete the sentences.

> ## Word Bank
>
> mittens   shorts   bathing suit
>
> jacket   umbrella   cap

1. I wear _____ on my hands when it is cold.

2. In the summer, I go swimming in my _____.

3. I carry an _____ in the spring in case it rains.

4. In the fall, I wear a _____ when the weather gets cool.

5. I must wear a _____ on my head to stay warm in the winter.

6. _____ help keep me cool on hot summer days.

Different Types of Houses

Directions: Look at each picture. Write the name of the type of house on the line. Use the Word Bank to help you.

Word Bank			
adobe	apartment	stilts	houseboat
log cabin	igloo	stucco	motorhome

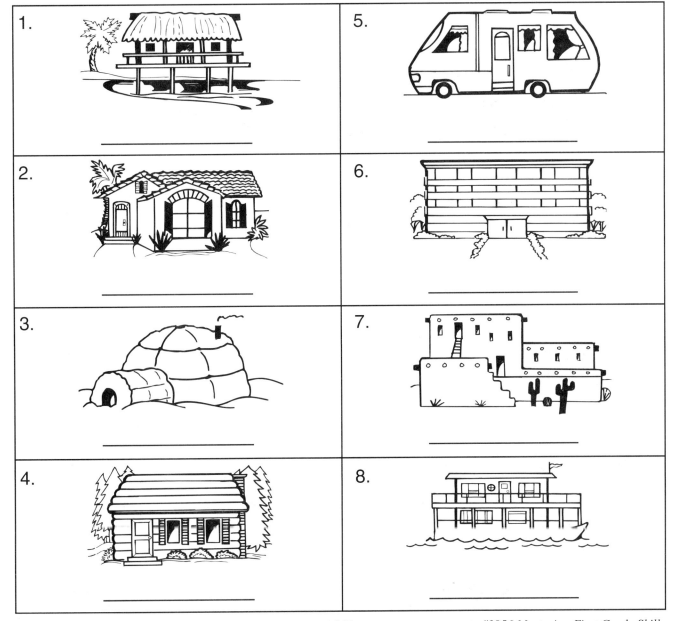

1. _____

2. _____

3. _____

4. _____

5. _____

6. _____

7. _____

8. _____

Compass Rose

Directions: Label the **compass points**. Use the Word Bank below to help you spell the words.

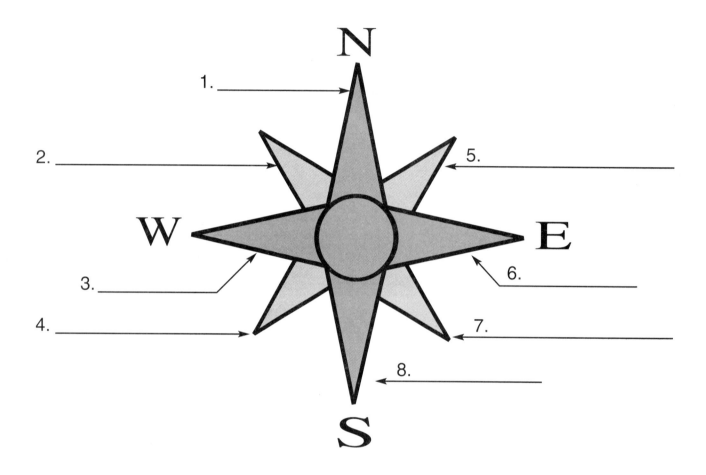

Word Bank

North	West	South–West
South	North–West	South–East
East	North–East	

Directions Quiz!

Directions: Answer these questions about **directions**.

1. What are the four main directions?

   _____ _____ _____ _____

2. What directions are opposite from each other?

   _____ is the opposite of _____

   _____ is the opposite of _____

3. If a map is drawn on a piece of paper, what direction is:

   at the top of the page? _____

   at the bottom of the page? _____

   on the left side of the page? _____

   on the right side of the page? _____

4. In the box to the right, label the arrows with the directions that show a picture of what you wrote to answer question #3.

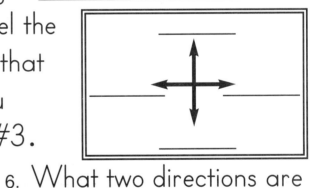

5. What two directions are next to west?

   __north__ _____

6. What two directions are next to east?

   _____ _____

7. What two directions are next to south?

   _____ __east__

8. What two directions are next to north?

   _____ _____

Which Way Should We Go?

Directions: Can you help the child find the playground? Tell him how many steps he should take **north, south, east, and west.** The first footprint is the first step.

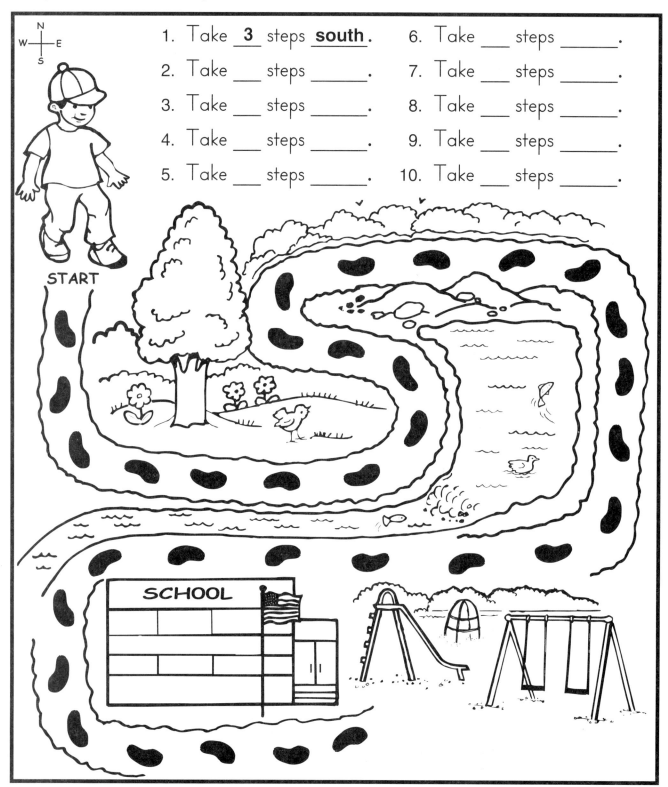

1. Take __3__ steps **south**.
2. Take ___ steps _____.
3. Take ___ steps _____.
4. Take ___ steps _____.
5. Take ___ steps _____.
6. Take ___ steps _____.
7. Take ___ steps _____.
8. Take ___ steps _____.
9. Take ___ steps _____.
10. Take ___ steps _____.

START

SCHOOL

Map Symbols

Directions: Draw a line to match each **symbol** to a word for its proper location.

1.  railroad

2.  airport

3. 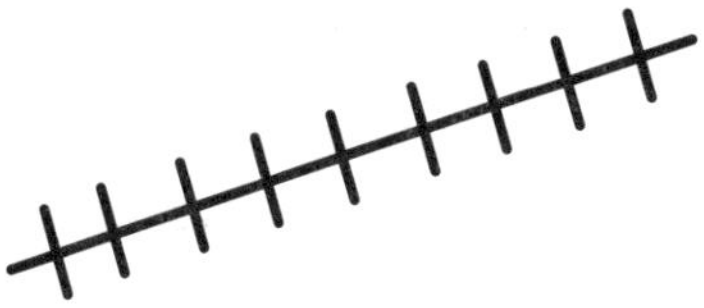 park

4. 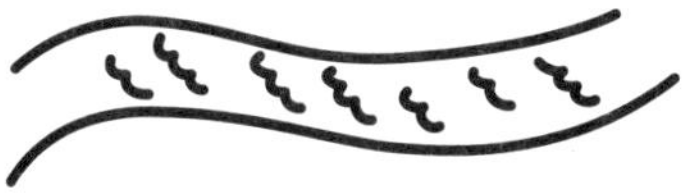 school

5.  road

6.  river

7.  hospital

8.  factory

You Make the Key!

Directions: Read the map on this page. Then draw the correct symbols next to each word in the **key**.

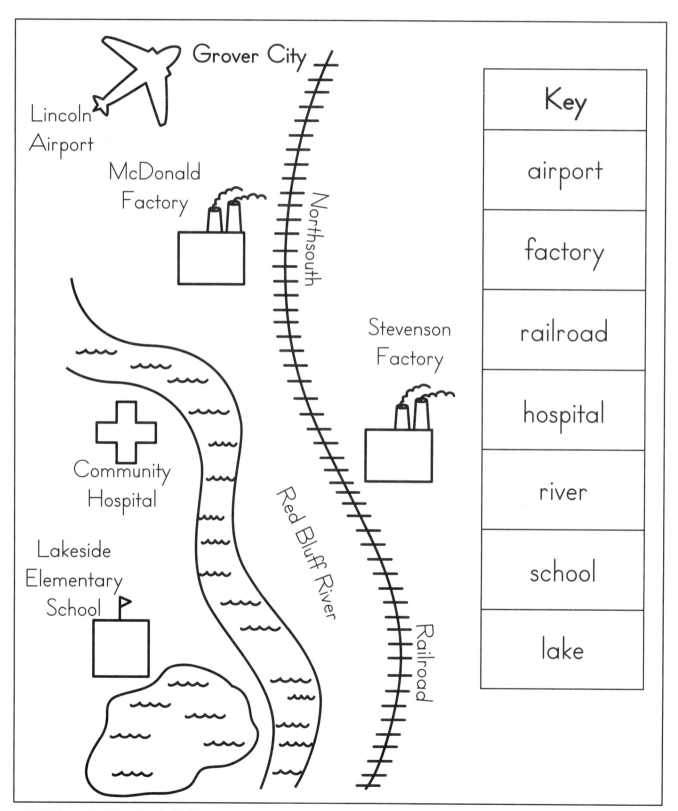

North, South, East, or West

Directions: Use the **map** to complete the sentences below. Circle the correct answer, then write it in the space provided.

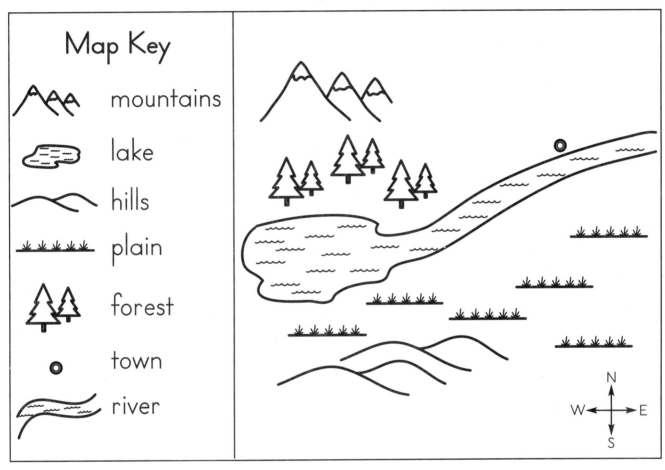

Map Key

mountains

lake

hills

plain

forest

town

river

Little Town

1. The town is _____ of the forest. (North South East West)

2. The lake is _____ of the river. (North South East West)

3. The river is _____ of the mountains. (North South East West)

4. The town is _____ of the plain. (North South East West)

5. The forest is _____ of the river. (North South East West)

6. The hills are _____ of the plain. (North South East West)

Your Map

Directions: Follow the directions at the bottom of the page in order to complete the map below. The first one has been done for you.

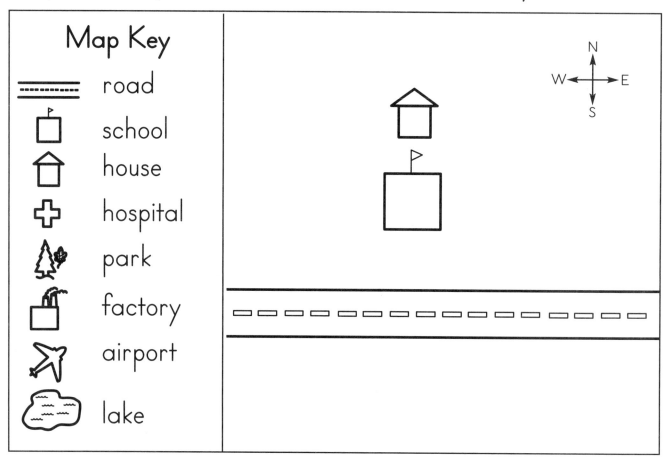

1. Draw a school **south** of the house.

2. Draw a park **west** of the school.

3. Draw a hospital **west** of the park.

4. Draw a lake **south** of the road.

5. Draw a park **east** of the lake.

6. Draw another house **east** of the house already on the map.

7. Draw a factory and explain where it is _____

Continents and Oceans

Directions: Write the names of the **seven continents** and the **four oceans** in the spaces below.

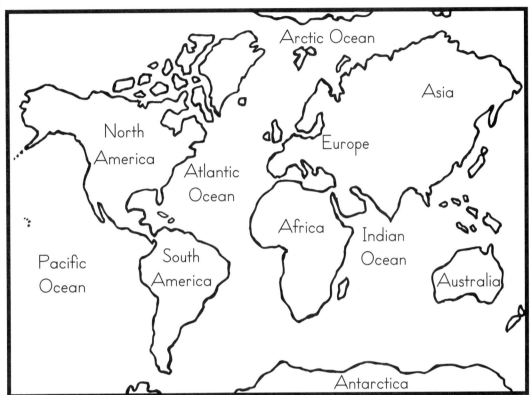

Continents

1. _____
2. _____
3. _____
4. _____
5. _____
6. _____
7. _____

Oceans

1. _____
2. _____
3. _____
4. _____

On which continent do you live? _____

Which ocean is closest to your location? _____

Our Country's Neighbors

Directions: Answer the questions. Color the **countries** as shown.

1. What is the name of the country in which you live?

   _____

   Color the United States blue.

2. What is the name of the country to the north of the United States?_____

   Color Canada red.

3. What is the name of the country to the south of the United States?_____

   Color Mexico green.

The Pledge of Allegiance

Directions: Use the words from the Word Bank to complete the **Pledge of Allegiance**. Then, using a dictionary, write a definition for the word at the bottom of the page.

Word Bank		
America	liberty	republic
Nation	flag	justice

The Pledge of Allegiance

I pledge allegiance to the _____,

of the United States of _____

and to the _____, for which

it stands, one _____ under

God, indivisible with _____

and _____ for all.

liberty _____

_____

George Washington

Directions: Read the passage below. Complete the sentences at the bottom of the page.

George Washington was born in 1732. As a young man, George Washington's job was to make maps. During this time, America was still a colony of England. Many people wanted America to be a separate country, free from England. They fought a war against England to gain their freedom. Washington was the general in charge of the Army during the war. When the war was over, the people wanted George Washington to be their first president. He served as president for eight years. The capital of the United States, Washington, D.C., was named in honor of him. George Washington was called the "Father of our Country." The Washington Monument was built to help us remember him.

1. George Washington was born in the year_____.

2. George Washington was the _____ of the Army during the war.

3. George Washington was elected the _____ president of the United States.

4. The capital of the United States is _____ D.C. It was named for him.

5. George Washington is called the _____.

Abraham Lincoln

Directions: Read the passage below. Answer the questions at the bottom of the page. Use complete sentences.

Abraham Lincoln was born on February 12, 1809. As a child, he loved to read books. He borrowed books from other people. Abraham Lincoln became the 16th president in 1860. The Civil War began while he was president. It lasted for four years. During the war, Lincoln worked to keep our country together. Abraham Lincoln was killed five days after the war ended. The people of the United States were very sad. They had lost their president. Lincoln will always be remembered. Many people believe that he was one of our greatest presidents. The Lincoln Memorial honors him today.

1. When was Abraham Lincoln born? _____

2. What did Abraham Lincoln borrow from other people? _____

3. When was Abraham Lincoln elected president of the United States? _____

4. What did Lincoln do during the war? _____

5. How do we honor Lincoln today? _____

The United States Flag

Directions: Complete the sentences below.

1. The colors of the United States flag are _____, white, and _____.

2. The stars are white on a _____ background.

3. There are _____ stars, one for each _____.

4. The _____ are white and red.

5. There are _____ stripes.

Now, color the U.S. flag.

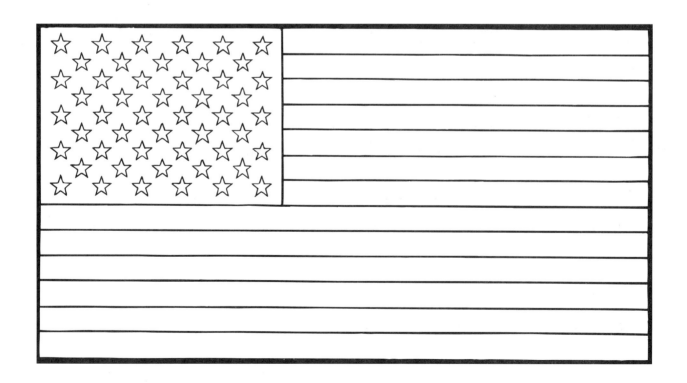

National Symbols Riddles

Directions: Use the words from the Word Bank below to answer the following National Symbol Riddles.

Word Bank

U.S. Flag	"The Star-Spangled Banner"
Statue of Liberty	Mount Rushmore
Pledge of Allegiance	Bald Eagle

1. I am the promise that Americans make to be loyal to our country. What am I? _____

2. I was carved on the side of a mountain in South Dakota. What am I? _____

3. I was presented to the United States by France. I stand in New York Harbor. What am I? _____

4. I am the national anthem. What am I? _____

5. I am called "Old Glory." What am I? _____

6. I am seen as a symbol of freedom. What am I? _____

Martin Luther King, Jr.

Directions: Use the words from the Word Bank to complete the sentences below about **Martin Luther King Jr.**

Word Bank

I have a dream	minister	leader	dream	1929
Coretta	Prize	fairly	holiday	laws

---

1. Martin Luther King Jr. was a famous American
   _____ who worked for change.

2. He was born in Georgia in_____ .

3. Even as a boy, Martin noticed that all people were not
   treated_____ . He started to think about how he
   could help.

4. He went to college and became a _____ .

5. Martin married a woman named _____ .

6. He worked to change unjust _____ . He gave
   speeches and led protests.

7. Dr. King made his most famous speech that began with the
   words, " _____ ."

8. Dr. King was given the Nobel Peace _____ for his
   work.

9. We have a _____ called Martin Luther
   King, Jr. Day.

10. We honor Dr. King each year to remember his
    _____ .

Timeline of My Life

Directions: Think of one major event that occurred during each year of your life. Draw a picture and write a caption to illustrate each event. If you have not turned 7 or 8 yet, think of something you want to do at those ages and ask an adult for assistance.

Birth	1 year old	2 years old
3 years old	4 years old	5 years old
6 years old	7 years old	8 years old

Long Ago and Today

Directions: Decide if the items below were popular long ago or today. Write the name of the item in the correct column.

 telephone

 camera

 electric car

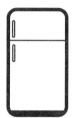 refrigerator

 CD player

 quill

 covered wagon

 butter churn

 computer

 cell phone

Long Ago	Today
1. _____	6. _____
2. _____	7. _____
3. _____	8. _____
4. _____	9. _____
5. _____	10. _____

Goods and Services

Directions: Look at each picture. Decide whether it is showing a **good** or a **service**. Circle the correct word.

1. good   service

2. good   service

3. good   service

4. good   service

5. good   service

6. good   service

7. CAR WASH
good   service

8. good   service

9. Good morning!
good   service

10. good   service

11. good   service

12. good   service

States of Matter

Directions: Look at each picture. Decide whether it is showing a **solid, liquid,** or **gas**. Circle the correct word.

1. solid

   liquid

   gas

2. solid

   liquid

   gas

3. solid

   liquid

   gas

4. solid

   liquid

   gas

5. solid

   liquid

   gas

6. solid

   liquid

   gas

7. solid

   liquid

   gas

8. solid

   liquid

   gas

9. solid

   liquid

   gas

10. solid

    liquid

    gas

Matter

Directions: Use the words from the Word Bank to complete the sentences below.

Word Bank

spread	forms	matter	container
described	wet	shape	solids

---

1. _____ is anything that takes up space.

2. Matter can be _____ by color, shape, size, or texture.

3. Matter can be found in three main _____.

4. Liquids are _____.

5. Liquids take the shape of the _____ they are in.

6. _____ have their own shape.

7. Solids do not change their _____ when they are moved.

8. Gases float around and _____ out.

Plant Parts

Directions: Use the words from the Word Bank to label the parts of the plant.

Word Bank

roots	flower	leaf	stem	seed

1. _____

2. _____

3. _____

4. _____

5. _____

What Parts Do We Eat?

Directions: Read the names of the foods below. Decide what part of the plant we eat. Write the **plant part** on the line.

| leaf | roots | stem | flower | seeds |

1. carrot	2. broccoli	3. beet
4. lettuce	5. radish	6. sunflower
7. cauliflower	8. spinach	9. asparagus
10. artichoke	11. potato	12. celery

Plant Part Functions

Directions: Use the words from the Word Bank to complete the sentences below.

Word Bank			
roots	leaves	grow	leaves
plant	stem	flower	seed

1. Plant a _____ to grow a plant.

2. Plants need water, soil, and sunlight in order to _____.

3. The _____ take water from the soil for the plant.

4. The roots help hold the _____ in place.

5. The stem helps hold up the _____.

6. A _____ brings water up the plant.

7. _____ make food for the plant.

8. The _____ has new seeds.

What Kind of Animal?

Directions: Look at each picture. Fill in the bubble to tell what kind of **animal** it is.

1.	⬭ bird	◯ reptile	◯ mammal
2.	◯ mammal	◯ insect	◯ bird
3.	◯ bird	◯ mammal	◯ fish
4.	◯ bird	◯ insect	◯ fish
5.	◯ insect	◯ fish	◯ mammal
6.	◯ mammal	◯ bird	◯ reptile
7.	◯ bird	◯ reptile	◯ mammal
8.	◯ mammal	◯ insect	◯ reptile

Animal Body Coverings

Directions: Look at each picture. Think about the animal. Decide what kind of **body covering** it has. Circle the correct word.

1. hair scales feathers	2. hair scales feathers	3. hair scales feathers
4. hair scales feathers	5. hair scales feathers	6. hair scales feathers
7. hair scales feathers	8. hair scales feathers	9. hair scales feathers
10. hair scales feathers	11. hair scales feathers	12. hair scales feathers

Animal Features

Directions: Use the words from the Word Bank to complete the sentences below.

Word Bank				
fish	segmented	fur	exoskeleton	feathers
milk	eggs	skin	fly	gills

1. Mammals have hair or _____. Babies feed on _____ from their mother's body.

2. Birds have _____, wings, two feet, and a hard beak. Most birds can _____.

3. Reptiles have scaly _____. Most reptiles lay _____.

4. _____ live in water. They have scales, fins, and _____.

5. Insects have _____ bodies. They have an _____.

The Water Cycle

Directions: Label the parts of the **water cycle**. Use the words from the Word Bank.

Word Bank

evaporation	condensation	rain	run-off

2. _____

1. _____

3. _____

4. _____

Describing the Water Cycle

Directions: Use the words from the Word Bank to complete the sentences below.

Word Bank

sun	condenses	rain	water cycle
runs off	evaporates	clouds	ocean

---

1. Water on earth collects in puddles, lakes, and in the _____.

2. The _____ warms the earth's water.

3. Water changes from a liquid to water vapor when it _____.

4. When water vapor cools, it _____.

5. Condensed water forms _____ high in the sky.

6. When the clouds become too heavy, they drop water as _____.

7. Rain water _____ to collect in puddles, lakes, and the ocean.

8. The changes of water are called the _____.

Answer Key

Page 8 *Beginning Sounds*
1. n   7. s   12. w
2. t   8. p   13. z
3. b   9. h   14. k
4. m   10. r   15. r
5. c   11. f   16. d
6. l

Page 9 *Which Beginning Sound?*
1. v   7. g   12. t
2. c   8. y   13. r
3. d   9. j   14. s
4. q   10. l   15. f
5. p   11. m   16. w
6. b

Page 10 *Change the Sound*
1. man   4. net   7. mop
2. hat   5. pig   8. bug
3. ten   6. pin

Page 11 *Change the Beginning Sound*
1. hat   4. get   7. dig
2. dog   5. sad   8. ten
3. sun   6. man

Page 12 *Add an Ending Sound*
1. sun   sub
2. pig   pin
3. web   wet
4. cat   can
5. man   map
6. dog   dot
7. bug   bun
8. bag   bat

Page 13 *Beginning and Ending Sounds*
1. bat   5. log   9. tub
2. pig   6. cat   10. bed
3. men   7. mop   11. fan
4. sun   8. pin   12. dog

Page 14 *Which Position?*
1. middle   11. ending
2. beginning   12. beginning
3. middle   13. ending
4. beginning   14. beginning
5. beginning   15. middle
6. middle   16. beginning
7. ending   17. ending
8. middle   18. beginning
9. middle   19. middle
10. beginning 20. beginning

Page 15 *Middle Sounds*
1. fan   fin
2. cot   cat
3. pin   pan
4. map   mop
5. net   nut
6. dig   dog
7. leg   log
8. bug   bag

Page 16 *Unscramble the Words*
1. cat   5. sit
2. mud   6. map
3. ten   7. jet
4. van   8. mop

Page 17 *Where in the Word?*
1. Beginning Consonant Words—
duck, fall, milk, nut, play, sack
Middle Consonant Words—ladder,
gift, camel, ring, apple, vest
Final Consonant Words—lid, leaf,
gum, rain, cup, bus

Page 18 *Beginning to End*
1. top   pot
2. gum   mug
3. net   ten
4. pan   nap
5. bat   tab
6. bus   sub

Page 19 *Add a Letter*
1. swing   5. bring
2. twig   6. spot
3. clock   7. brain
4. slip   8. stop

Page 20 *Delete a Letter*
1. oat   4. an   7. in
2. at   5. itch 8. ice
3. and   6. ox

Page 21 *Short Aa Crossword*

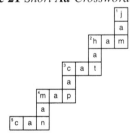

Page 22 *Short Ee Pictures*
1. short e
2. not short e
3. not short e
4. short e
5. not short e
6. short e
7. short e
8. not short e
9. short e
10. short e
11. short e

12. not short e
13. short e
14. short e
15. not short e
16. short e

Page 23 *Crossing Short Ii Words*
1. pig   5. pin
2. lip   6. sit
3. dig   7. rip
4. fin   8. kit

Page 24 *Short Oo Words*
1. box, o
2. dot, o
3. hop, o
4. sock, o
5. log, o
6. mop, o
7. dog, o
8. pot, o
9. hop or mop
10. pot or dot
11. sock
12. dog or log
13. dog or log
14. mop or hop
15. box
16. pot or dot

Page 25 *Short Uu Word Search*
1. sun   5. tug   9. sub
2. bug   6. hug   10. rug
3. tub   7. run   11. cub
4. bun   8. jug   12. mug

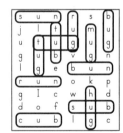

Page 26 *Short Aa, Ii, and Uu*
1. dad   did
2. ham   him
3. slam   slim
4. ban   bin
5. bat   bit
6. pan   pin
7. fan   fin
8. bag   big
9. rag   rig
10. lamp   limp

Short **Aa** Words – bad, jam, can, fat
Short **Ii** Words – hit, drip, twig, win
Short **Uu** Words – nut, run, cub, plug

Answer Key *(cont.)*

Page 27 *Which Short Vowel?*
1. sun   4. tub   7. fin
2. mat   5. cub   8. hen
3. net   6. dig

Page 28 *Long Aa*
1. tail   4. cage   7. paid
2. bake   5. wait   8. face
3. cape   6. hay

Page 29 *Long Ee*
Answers will vary. Students should have followed the directions to draw a picture.

Page 30 *Long iI*

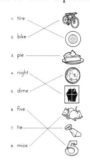

1. tire
2. bike
3. pie
4. night
5. dime
6. five
7. tie
8. mice

Page 31 *Long Oo*
1. stone, tone, throne, alone, cone
2. low, now, snow, row
3. moat, coat, vote, boat, float
4. bold, hold, cold, told, fold

Page 32 *Long Uu*
1. June   5. tuba
2. Utah   6. tune
3. uniforms   7. duet
4. flute

Page 33 *Magic Ee*
1. tap   4. cube   7. can   9. kit
2. tape   5. tub   8. cane 10. kite
3. cub   6. tube

Page 34 *Short or Long?*
1. short, o   9. short, i
2. long, i   10. long, a
3. short, u   11. short, a
4. long, o   12. short, o
5. long, u   13. short, e
6. short, o   14. short, i
7. long, e   15. long, o
8. short, u   16. short, i

Page 35 *Long and Short Vowel Train Cars*
2. tree, pen   4. note, dog
3. nine, pig   5. flute, sun

Page 36 *Long and Short Vowel Sort*
Short A—cab, plan, snap
Short E—best, yet, fed
Short I—stick, swing, rip
Short O—dock, spot, fog
Short U—stub, plug, cut
Long A—blame, grape, take

Long E—green, leap, eel
Long I—bride, line, like
Long O—boat, note, woke
Long U—suit, juice, glue

Page 37 *Rr, Ll, and Ss Blends*
1. br   8. gl   15. st
2. gr   9. cl   16. sl
3. pr   10. fl   17. sk
4. cr   11. pl   18. sm
5. fr   12. cl   19. sp
6. br   13. gl   20. st
7. tr   14. bl   21. sq

Page 38 *Sorting Rr, Ll, and Ss Blends*
Rr Blends – dragon, frame, bridge, present, crown, truck, grape, crib
Ll Blends – plant, globe, clam, clap, play, glue, block, flame
Ss Blends – swing, stone, star, sponge, swim, smoke, spider, stop

Page 39 *Ending Blends*
1. sk   5. mp   9. mp   12. nk
2. st   6. nk   10. ng   13. st
3. lm   7. nt   11. mp   14. mp
4. sk   8. sk

Page 40 *Identifying Digraphs*
2. ch, ending
3. th, middle
4. th, ending
5. sh, ending
6. ch, ending
7. sh, beginning
8. ch, middle
9. wh, beginning
10. th, beginning
11. th, ending
12. wh, beginning

Page 41 *Controlled Rr Words*
1. shark   5. tractor   9. letter
2. bird   6. river   10. turkey
3. corn   7. nurse   11. thirteen
4. horse   8. star   12. yarn
    ar words – shark, star, yarn
    er words – river, letter
    ir words – bird, thirteen
    or words – tractor, corn, horse
    ur words – turkey, nurse

Page 42 *Word Endings*
1. jumps, jumped, jumping
2. mows, mowed, mowing
3. cooks, cooked, cooking
4. opens, opened, opening
5. answers, answered, answering
6. pick

7. crash
8. smile
9. go
10. look
11. help
12. talk
13. play
14. love
15. see

Page 43 *Words in a Family*
1. fan, can, van
2. fin, pin, win
3. jet, net, vet
4. hand, sand, band
5. mop, pop, hop

Page 44 *Rhyming Sentences*
1. book   4. hat   7. bee
2. box   5. truck 8. bike
3. frog   6. fish

Page 45 *Sorting Word Families*
1. net   4. cot   7. jet   10. wet
2. map   5. bug   8. mug   11. rug
3. pot   6. tap   9. dot   12. cap
    -ap words—map, tap, cap
    -et words—net, jet, wet
    -ot words—pot, cot, dot
    -ug words—bug, mug, rug

Page 46 *Synonym Find*
1. hog   4. shut   7. speak
2. glad   5. mad   8. home
3. chilly   6. loud

Page 47 *Antonym Crossword*

Page 48 *Opposite Sentences*
1. awake, asleep   4. big, small
2. close, open   5. up, down
3. hot, cold   6. won, lost

Page 49 *Synonyms or Antonyms*
1. synonyms   7. antonyms
2. antonyms   8. synonyms
3. synonyms   9. antonyms
4. antonyms   10. synonyms
5. antonyms   11. antonyms
6. antonyms   12. antonyms

Answer Key *(cont.)*

Page 50 *Synonyms and Antonyms Sort*
1. ill, well
2. alike, different
3. large, small
4. quick, slow
5. smile, frown
6. arrive, leave

Page 51 *Sounds the Same, Spelled Differently*
1. ate
2. pare
3. son
4. right
5. sale
6. not
7. flour
8. ant
9. tale
10. be
11. would
12. to

Page 52 *Homonym Sentences*
1. He ate eight grapes.
2. I need to knead the dough.
3. I wrote a tale about my dog's tail.
4. She knew I got a new car.
5. I got dirt in my eye.
6. Do you write with your right hand?
7. I have four flowers for you.
8. The button fell off so I had to sew it back on.

Page 53 *Two Meanings*
1. bat
2. pot
3. saw
4. orange
5. top
6. bowl

Page 54 *Make a Compound Word*
1. doghouse
2. seashell
3. teapot
4. rainbow
5. football

Page 55 *Compound Word Sentences*
1. doghouse
2. snowman
3. seashell
4. bluebird
5. beehive
6. doorbell
7. bedroom
8. teapot

Page 56 *Animal ABC Order*
1. bird, cat, dog, lizard
2. elephant, giraffe, lion, tiger
3. cow, horse, pig, sheep
4. crab, fish, octopus, shark

Page 57 *Fruits and Vegetables ABC Order*
Fruits—apple, banana, cherry, orange, pear, plum
Vegetables—bean, carrot, lettuce, pea, potato, squash

Page 58 *Same Letter ABC Order*
1. dance, deer, dinosaur, doll, drive
2. gate, glue, goat, grape, gum
3. math, melt, milk, monkey, mud
4. sail, slide, smell, snake, soft

Page 59 *Person, Place, or Thing?*
1. person—Dad, place—park, thing—bike
2. person—children, place—theater, thing—song
3. person—children, place—pool, thing—bathing suits
4. person—queen, place—castle, thing—crown
5. person—boy, place—library, thing—book

Page 60 *Naming Common Nouns*
Words in the Proper Noun columns will vary. Check to ensure, students named a specific person, place or thing. Answers provided below are for the third column.
1. place
2. person
3. place
4. place
5. person
6. thing
7. person
8. place

Page 61 *More Than One*
1. pig, pigs
2. snake, snakes
3. dog, dogs
4. horse, horses
5. bird, birds
6. rabbit, rabbits
7. bug, bugs
8. cat, cats

Page 62 *Action Words*
1. chased
2. twinkles
3. watched
4. set
5. swim
6. sings
7. eat
8. threw

Page 63 *Action Sentences*
Answers provided below are for the first column. Ensure sentences in the second column include the verb and are complete.
1. picking
2. jumping
3. riding
4. sleeping
5. swimming
6. throwing
7. eating
8. mowing

Page 64 *Describe It*
1. big
2. smelly
3. three
4. beautiful
5. quiet
6. hot
7. cute
8. round

Page 65 *How Many? What Kind?*
Student answers will vary for second column. Answers provided below are for the first column.1
1. one
2. two
3. twelve
4. six
5. one
6. three
7. four
8. one

Page 66 *A Descriptive Story*
Student answers may vary in order to make very silly sentences. Possible answers are listed below.
1. warm
2. spiky
3. red, blue
4. scrambled, two
5. orange
6. best

Page 67 *Pronoun Party*
1. us
2. them
3. We
4. It
5. he
6. They
7. their
8. his
9. she
10. I

Page 68 *Parts of Speech Review*
Nouns—flowers, sun, children, ball, ducks
Verbs—running, hopping, skating, swimming
Adjectives—two, round, happy, bright, beautiful

Page 69 *Which Contraction?*
1. I'm
2. We're
3. isn't
4. can't
5. we'll
6. shouldn't
7. isn't
8. it's

Page 70 *Making Contractions*
1. it's
2. let's
3. he'll
4. aren't
5. you'd
6. can't
7. she's
8. didn't
9. you're

Page 71 *Finding Contractions*
2. could, not
3. we, are
4. you, would
5. it, is
6. they, are
7. can, not
8. he, is
9. would, not
10. I, am

Page 72 *Statement or Question?*
1. period
2. period
3. question mark
4. period
5. period
6. question mark
7. period
8. period

Page 73 *Write a Question*
Student's answers will vary. Ensure student's sentences are questions and end with a question mark.

Page 74 *End It Right*
1. ?
2. .
3. .
4. !
5. .
6. ?
7. .
8. !
9. .
10. .

Answer Key

Page 75 *First Words*
1. My   4. We   7. Are
2. Can   5. She   8. Her
3. I   6. There

Page 76 *Name It*
Students' answers will vary. Ensure students completed each sentence with a proper noun and that they capitalized the noun.

Page 77 *Where Do You Live?*
Student's answers will vary, depending on where they live. Check for accuracy and capitalization of the proper nouns.

Page 78 *Capitalization*
1. California
2. Sunshine Hotel
3. Tuesday
4. Pacific Ocean
5. I
6. Sally
7. Shake Shack
8. We

Page 79 *Scrambled Sentences*
1. The dog is so cute.
2. She just had eight puppies.
3. There were two black puppies.
4. Five were brown puppies.
5. What was the color of the last one?

Page 80 *Complete Sentences*
1. complete   4. complete
2. complete   5. incomplete
3. incomplete
Students should use #3 and #5 to write complete sentences.

Page 81 *Writing Complete Sentences*
Students should choose one word from each column to write sentences. Ensure students' sentences make sense and that they begin with a capital letter and end with a period.

Page 82 *Make a Sentence*
Students should choose one word from each column to write sentences. Ensure students' sentences make sense and that they begin with a capital letter and end with a period.

Page 83 *Create a Sentence*
Students' sentences will vary. Ensure students' sentences make sense.

Page 84 *Answer the Question*
Students' answers will vary. Ensure students' sentences make sense and that they begin with a capital letter and end with a period.

Page 85 *Changing Questions into Statements*
Students should change the questions into statements. Answers may vary. Suggested answers are provided below.
1. She likes to sing.
2. Mark cleaned his room.
3. The dog is nice.
4. Sarah plays the piano.
5. They liked the movie.

Page 86 *Changing Statements into Questions*
Students should change the statements into questions. Answers may vary. Suggested answers are provided below.
1. Does Mike have any pets?
2. Who does she love?
3. What did you have for lunch?
4. What did Mom make?
5. What does Louie like to do?

Page 87 *Adding Adjectives to Sentences*
Students' answers may vary. Suggested answers are provided below.
1. little
2. interesting
3. tall, green
4. big
5. beautiful
6. comfortable
7. white, orange
8. fuzzy

Page 88 *Expanding Sentences*
Students' answers will vary. Ensure students added two more words to expand each sentence.

Page 89 *Create a Story*
Students' answers will vary. Ensure students' stories have the characters, settings, objects, and situations that were checked at the top of their page.

Page 90 *What Is It?*
Students' stories will vary.

Page 91 *Who Lives Here?*
Students' stories will vary.

Page 92 *Marooned*
Students' stories will vary.

Page 93 *Octopus Bath*
Students' stories will vary.

Page 94 *Observing a Banana*
Students' observations will vary.

Page 95 *Sequencing Events*
Students' answers will vary.

Page 96 *Real or Make Believe?*
1. real
2. make believe
3. real
4. make believe
5. make believe
6. real
7. real
8. make believe

Page 97 *Predicting*
1. decorate the house with balloons.
2. rinses and dries the dog.
3. puts them in the oven.

Page 98 *Fact or Opinion?*
1. fact   6. fact
2. opinion   7. opinion
3. fact   8. fact
4. opinion   9. fact
5. opinion   10. opinion

Page 99 *Word Use*
1. b   3. a   5. a
2. b   4. b   6. a

Page 100 *Sequencing*
The sequence of #2, #3, and #4 may vary. Suggested answers are provided below.
1. The new pony lay quietly on the ground.
2. She put her front hooves on the grass.
3. She lifted her nose into the air.
4. Her wobbly legs pushed her up.
5. The new pony was standing on her own!

Page 101 *Main Idea*
1. seasons
2. fruit
3. instruments
4. clothes
5. writing tools
6. colors
7. numbers
8. months

Page 102 *Supporting Details*
Shapes—circle, square, triangle, rectangle
Buildings—library, bank, school, house
Instruments—piano, violin, drums, tuba
Transportation—motorcycle, plane, ship, car

Page 103 *Categorizing*
Students' answers will vary. Ensure students' answers match the category.

Answer Key *(cont.)*

Page 104 *Inferring*
1. b   3. a   5. c
2. c   4. b

Page 105 *Penguins*
1. b   3. a
2. b   4. c

Page 106 *Best Friends*
Students' sentences may vary, but should include the information from the sample sentences below.
1. Marta and Janis are friends.
2. The girls do their homework.
3. They go to the park.
4. Marta skates and Janis rides her scooter.
5. Answers will vary.

Page 107 *Giraffes*
1. b   3. c   5. b   2. a   4. a

Page 108 *Connect the Dots*

Page 109 *Connect the Dots*

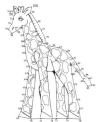

Page 110 *Counting to 100*

1	2	3	4	5	6	7	8	9	10
11	12	13	14	15	16	17	18	19	20
21	22	23	24	25	26	27	28	29	30
31	32	33	34	35	36	37	38	39	40
41	42	43	44	45	46	47	48	49	50
51	52	53	54	55	56	57	58	59	60
61	62	63	64	65	66	67	68	69	70
71	72	73	74	75	76	77	78	79	80
81	82	83	84	85	86	87	88	89	90
91	92	93	94	95	96	97	98	99	100

Page 111 *Count, Write, Name*
1. 6, six   6. 3, three
2. 2, two   7. 1, one
3. 7, seven   8. 5, five
4. 9, nine   9. 10, ten
5. 4, four   10. 8, eight

Page 112 *Number Name Picture*

Page 113 *Larger Number Names*
1. 72   6. 87
2. 16   7. 4
3. 41   8. 56
4. 38   9. 65
5. 23

    4, 16, 23, 38, 41, 56, 65, 72, 87

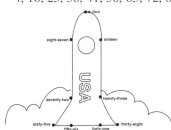

Page 114 *Counting Tens and Ones*
1. 2 tens 5 ones, 25
2. 3 tens 4 ones, 34
3. 5 tens 8 ones, 58
4. 1 ten 5 ones, 15
5. 6 tens 0 ones, 60
6. 0 tens 6 ones, 6
7. 4 tens 8 ones, 48
8. 4 tens 5 ones, 45

Page 115 *Counting Balls*
1. 4   7. 25
2. 11   8. 34
3. 20   9. 13
4. 21   10. 32
5. 31   11. 16
6. 35   12. 30

Page 116 *Writing Numbers in Expanded Notation*
2. 40 + 7
3. 90 + 6
4. 60 + 3
5. 30 + 9
6. 20 + 4
7. 80 + 1
8. 10 + 7
9. 0 + 4
10. 70 + 5
11. 50 + 3 = 53
    50 + 4 = 54
    50 + 5 = 55

12. 70 + 8 = 78
    70 + 9 = 79
    70 + 10 = 80

Page 117 *Find the Numbers*
1. 43, 41, 49   5. 7, 8, 2
2. 19, 79, 9, 29   6. 100
3. 25   7. 40, 90, 100
4. 60, 30   8. 5, 30, 50, 65

Page 118 *Make a Number*
1. largest 52, smallest 25
2. largest 95, smallest 59
3. largest 63, smallest 36
4. largest 75, smallest 57
5. largest 84, smallest 48
6. largest 96, smallest 69
7. largest 71, smallest 17
8. largest 43, smallest 34
9. largest 97, smallest 79
10. largest 82, smallest 28
11. largest 64, smallest 46
12. largest 81, smallest 18
13. largest 73 smallest 37,
14. largest 53, smallest 35
15. largest 50, smallest 5

Page 119 *Mystery Numbers*
1. 952   4. 267
2. 186   5. 398
3. 403   6. 100

Page 120 *Using Number Clues*
1. 73, seventy-three
2. 97, ninety-seven
3. 38, thirty-eight
4. 66, sixty-six
5. 14, fourteen
6. 40, forty
7. 5, five
8. 81, eighty-one
9. 27, twenty-seven
10. 59, fifty-nine

Answer Key *(cont.)*

Page 121 *More Number Clues*

1. 22 3. 72 5. 74 7. 53
2. 35 4. 10 6. 9 8. 46

Page 123 *Before, After, Between*

1. 15 13. 39
2. 28 14. 85
3. 66 15. 56
4. 47 16. 27
5. 34 17. 24
6. 71 18. 57
7. 52 19. 95
8. 88 20. 33
9. 20 21. 42
10. 94 22. 76
11. 63 23. 88,
12. 48 24. 17
Bonus 79

Page 124 *Sequencing Numbers*

1. 18, 21, 32, 43, 57
2. 25, 47, 51, 72, 98
3. 32, 49, 68, 74, 83
4. 27, 38, 49, 52, 75
5. 26, 33, 57, 76, 93
6. 17, 36, 52, 77, 94

Page 125 *Missing Apartment Numbers*

Row 1 (top row) 50, 51, 52, 53, 54
Row 2 40, 41, 42, 43, 44
Row 3 30, 32, 33, 34
Row 4 (bottom row) 20, 21, 22, 23, 24

Page 126 *Ten, More or Less*

1. 37, 57 6. 43, 63
2. 72, 92 7. 31, 51
3. 26, 46 8. 64, 84
4. 69, 89 9. 58, 78
5. 10, 30 10. 75, 95

Page 127 *Places Everyone*

1. 4th 4. 6th 7. Andrew
2. 5th 5. 3rd 8. Mary
3. 2nd 6. 1st 9. Daniel

Page 128 *Finish Line*

1. red 5. yellow 9. green
2. orange 6. blue 10. green
3. yellow 7. red
4. green 8. yellow

Page 129 *Numbers Large and Small*

1. 19 8. 57 15. 80
2. 81 9. 84 16. 27
3. 24 10. 43 17. 56
4. 37 11. 17 18. 81
5. 78 12. 32 19. 37
6. 58 13. 51 20. 16
7. 93 14. 75

Page 130 *Greater Than, Less Than*

1. < 6. > 11. >
2. > 7. > 12. <
3. < 8. = 13. =
4. > 9. < 14. <
5. < 10. > 15. >

Page 131 *Counting by 10s*

10, 20, 30, 40, 50, 60, 70, 80, 90, 100

Page 132 *Counting by 5s*

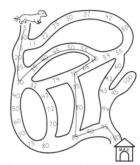

Page 133 *Counting by 2s*

1	2	3	4	5	6	7	8	9	10
11	12	13	14	15	16	17	18	19	20
21	22	23	24	25	26	27	28	29	30
31	32	33	34	35	36	37	38	39	40
41	42	43	44	45	46	47	48	49	50
51	52	53	54	55	56	57	58	59	60
61	62	63	64	65	66	67	68	69	70
71	72	73	74	75	76	77	78	79	80
81	82	83	84	85	86	87	88	89	90
91	92	93	94	95	96	97	98	99	100

There is a vertical line pattern with every other column shaded.

Page 134 *Counting Body Parts*

1. 14 4. 50 7. 4 10. 60
2. 8 5. 10 8. 8 11. 7
3. 7 6. 6 9. 9 12. 8

Page 135 *Skip Counting Problem Solving*

1. 10 + 10 + 10 + 10 = 40
   or 10, 20, 30, 40
2. 2 + 2 + 2 = 6
   or 2, 4, 6
3. 2 + 2 + 2 + 2 + 2 + 2 + 2 = 14
   or 2, 4, 6, 8, 10, 12, 14
4. 10 + 10 + 10 + 10 + 10 + 10 + 10 = 70
   or 10, 20, 30, 40, 50, 60, 70

Page 136 *Odd or Even*

1. even 5. odd 9. odd
2. odd 6. even 10. odd
3. even 7. odd 11. even
4. even 8. even 12. odd

2	90	38	46	88	12	92	44	68
92	3	22	23	66	17	87	1	4
56	15	98	11	36	45	16	91	24
58	57	39	75	6	27	59	73	54
8	72	50	29	62	78	100	69	10
40	48	26	47	14	32	52	37	48
18	96	70	96	86	38	20	42	80

odd mystery number 9
even mystery number 4

Page 137 *Show Addition*

1. 3 + 2 = 5
2. 6 + 1 = 7
3. 5 + 3 = 8
4. 4 + 2 = 6
5. 3 + 0 = 3
6. 4 + 4 = 8

Page 138 *Ways to Make 6*

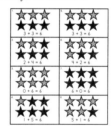

Page 139 *Addition Mystery Picture*

Page 140 *Ways to Equal a Sum*

1. 3 + 5, 7 + 1, 6 + 2
2. 2 + 2, 4 + 0, 3 + 1, 0 + 4
3. 6 + 0, 4 + 2, 3 + 3, 5 + 1
4. 2 + 0, 1 + 1, 0 + 2
5. 3 + 6, 1 + 8, 9 + 0
6. 3 + 0, 2 + 1, 0 + 3, 1 + 2
7. 6 + 1, 2 + 5, 4 + 3, 7 + 0
8. 5 + 0, 3 + 2, 1 + 4, 3 + 2

Answer Key (cont.)

Page 141 *Missing Addends*

1. 1   4. 3   7. 7   9. 8
2. 5   5. 2   8. 0   10. 6
3. 4   6. 10

Riddle Answer: To get to the other slide.

Page 142 *Equal on Both Sides*

1. 2   4. 0   7. 2   9. 8
2. 4   5. 6   8. 1   10. 9
3. 5   6. 7

Page 143 *Make Them Equal*

1. 3   4. 4   7. 4   9. 5
2. 3   5. 3   8. 1   10. 0
3. 3   6. 4

Challenge: 6

Page 144 *Writing Number Sentences*
Students' addition problems will vary.

Page 145 *Addition Wheels*

1. $5 + 4 = 9$
    $6 + 4 = 10$
    $7 + 4 = 11$
    $8 + 4 = 12$
    $9 + 4 = 13$
    $10 + 4 = 14$
    $11 + 4 = 15$
    $12 + 4 = 16$
2. $6 + 5 = 11$
    $7 + 5 = 12$
    $8 + 5 = 13$
    $9 + 5 = 14$
    $10 + 5 = 15$
    $11 + 5 = 16$
    $12 + 5 = 17$
    $13 + 5 = 18$
3. $4 + 6 = 10$
    $5 + 6 = 11$
    $6 + 6 = 12$
    $7 + 6 = 13$
    $8 + 6 = 14$
    $9 + 6 = 15$
    $10 + 6 = 16$
    $11 + 6 = 17$
4. $3 + 7 = 10$
    $4 + 7 = 11$
    $5 + 7 = 12$
    $6 + 7 = 13$
    $7 + 7 = 14$
    $8 + 7 = 15$
    $9 + 7 = 16$
    $10 + 7 = 17$
5. $2 + 8 = 10$
    $3 + 8 = 11$
    $4 + 8 = 12$
    $5 + 8 = 13$
    $6 + 8 = 14$

$7 + 8 = 15$
$8 + 8 = 16$
$9 + 8 = 17$
6. $1 + 9 = 10$
    $2 + 9 = 11$
    $3 + 9 = 12$
    $4 + 9 = 13$
    $5 + 9 = 14$
    $6 + 9 = 15$
    $7 + 9 = 16$
    $8 + 9 = 17$

Page 146 *Addition Crossword*

Page 147 *Adding 3 Numbers*

1. 10   4. 7   7. 9
2. 8   5. 11   8. 6
3. 12   6. 13   9. 14

Page 148 *Addition Word Problems*

1. $3 + 2 = 5$
    Tom has 5 toy cars.
2. $2 + 2 = 4$ or $1 + 1 + 1 + 1 = 4$
    There are 4 girls playing.
3. $8 + 5 = 13$
    Micah has 13 trading cards.
4. $2 + 5 = 7$
    Ryanna checked out 5 books from
    the city library.

Page 149 *Show Subtraction*

1. $5 - 2 = 31$ 4. $7 - 6 = 1$
2. $6 - 4 = 2$ 5. $5 - 5 = 0$
3. $4 - 1 = 3$ 6. $6 - 3 = 3$

Page 150 *Draw Subtraction*
Students' drawings will vary. Ensure
they have the correct number of
pictures drawn and then crossed off to
show the subtraction problem.

Page 151 *Odd or Even?*

1. 5, odd   9. 1, odd
2. 1, odd   10. 2, even
3. 5, odd   11. 2, even
4. 5, odd   12. 3, odd
5. 3, odd   13. 3, odd
6. 2, even   14. 3, odd
7. 4, even   15. 3, odd
8. 3, odd   16. 1, odd

Page 152 *Subtraction Machines*

1. $7 - 5 = 2$
    $9 - 5 = 4$
    $5 - 5 = 0$
    $6 - 5 = 1$
2. $4 - 3 = 1$
    $6 - 3 = 3$
    $5 - 3 = 2$
    $9 - 3 = 6$
3. $8 - 7 = 1$
    $7 - 7 = 0$
    $9 - 7 = 2$
    $10 - 7 = 3$
4. $6 - 6 = 0$
    $9 - 6 = 3$
    $8 - 6 = 2$
    $7 - 6 = 1$
5. $9 - 1 = 8$
    $4 - 1 = 3$
    $2 - 1 = 1$
    $6 - 1 = 5$
6. $5 - 4 = 1$
    $8 - 4 = 4$
    $4 - 4 = 0$
    $7 - 4 = 3$
7. $8 - 8 = 0$
    $10 - 8 = 2$
    $9 - 8 = 1$
    $11 - 8 = 3$
8. $3 - 2 = 1$
    $5 - 2 = 3$
    $7 - 2 = 5$
    $2 - 2 = 0$
9. $4 - 3 = 1$
    $9 - 3 = 6$
    $5 - 3 = 2$
    $8 - 3 = 5$

Page 153 *What's Missing?*

1. 2   4. 3   7. 5   9. 4
2. 3   5. 3   8. 3   10. 2
3. 8   6. 2

Page 154 *Subtraction Wheels*

1. $10 - 2 = 8$
    $8 - 2 = 6$
    $3 - 2 = 1$
    $6 - 2 = 4$
    $12 - 2 = 10$
    $5 - 2 = 3$
    $17 - 2 = 15$
    $4 - 2 = 2$
2. $9 - 5 = 4$
    $6 - 5 = 1$
    $11 - 5 = 6$
    $5 - 5 = 0$
    $10 - 5 = 5$
    $17 - 5 = 12$

Answer Key *(cont.)*

$7 - 5 = 2$
$13 - 5 = 8$
3. $10 - 3 = 7$
$5 - 3 = 2$
$7 - 3 = 4$
$11 - 3 = 8$
$15 - 3 = 12$
$3 - 3 = 0$
$9 - 3 = 6$
$6 - 3 = 3$
4. $4 - 4 = 0$
$8 - 4 = 4$
$12 - 4 = 8$
$17 - 4 = 13$
$9 - 4 = 5$
$13 - 4 = 9$
$7 - 4 = 3$
$15 - 4 = 11$
5. $17 - 6 = 11$
$9 - 6 = 3$
$7 - 6 = 1$
$12 - 6 = 6$
$10 - 6 = 4$
$15 - 6 = 9$
$6 - 6 = 0$
$11 - 6 = 5$
6. $2 - 1 = 1$
$19 - 1 = 18$
$9 - 1 = 8$
$13 - 1 = 12$
$10 - 1 = 9$
$4 - 1 = 3$
$7 - 1 = 6$
$15 - 1 = 14$

Page 155 *Subtraction Riddle*
1. 5   5. 11   9. 8
2. 9   6. 10   10. 9
3. 12   7. 13   11. 6
4. 7   8. 9   12. 12
If they lived by the bay, they would be called bagels.

Page 156 *Subtraction Word Problems*
1. $7 - 3 = 4$
Tyler made the basket 4 times.
2. $6 - 2 = 4$
Four children are left playing hockey.
3. $5 - 3 = 2$
Mandi ate 3 cookies.
4. $8 - 6 = 2$
Bernice has to do 2 more pages of homework.

Page 157 *How Many?*
1. There are 3 cookies in the bag.
2. There are 5 kittens in the box.

3. There are 10 pencils in the box.
4. There are 17 hangers in the closet.
5. There are 3 people in the house.

Page 158 *Addition and Subtraction Machines*
1. $12 - 4 = 8$
$8 - 4 = 4$
$20 - 4 = 16$
$15 - 4 = 11$
2. $9 + 6 = 15$
$12 + 6 = 18$
$7 + 6 = 13$
$2 + 6 = 8$
3. $17 - 8 = 9$
$11 - 8 = 3$
$20 - 8 = 12$
$15 - 8 = 7$
4. $14 + 3 = 17$
$9 + 3 = 12$
$17 + 3 = 20$
$4 + 3 = 7$
5. $14 + 5 = 19$
$3 + 5 = 8$
$12 + 5 = 17$
$9 + 5 = 14$
6. $15 - 5 = 10$
$9 - 5 = 4$
$18 - 5 = 13$
$6 - 5 = 1$
7. $19 - 6 = 13$
$13 - 6 = 7$
$9 - 6 = 3$
$6 - 6 = 0$
8. $19 + 1 = 20$
$15 + 1 = 16$
$3 + 1 = 4$
$9 + 1 = 10$
9. $8 - 4 = 4$
$17 - 4 = 13$
$5 - 4 = 1$
$13 - 4 = 9$

Page 159 *Addition and Subtraction Puzzle*
1. 7   7. 1   12. 7
2. 4   8. 7   13. 10
3. 6   9. 3   14. 2
4. 16   10. 12   15. 14
5. 7   11. 8   16. 19
6. 4

Page 160 *Farm Word Problems*
1. $4 + 8 = 12$
There are 12 pigs on the farm now.
2. $6 + 7 = 13$
There are 13 sheep on the farm.

3. $7 - 3 = 4$
The farmer gives away 4 kittens.
4. $5 + 7 + 6 = 18$
There are 18 cows on the farm.

Page 161 *Farm Word Problems, cont.*
5. $8 - 6 = 2$
There are 2 goats awake.
6. $7 - 2 = 5$
The farmer was able to plow his field 5 days this week.
7. $2 + 2 + 2 + 2 + 2 + 2 + 2 = 14$
The farmer has to milk the cows 14 times each week.
8. $9 - 6 = 3$
There are 3 ducks in the pond.

Page 162 *Missing Numbers*
1. $4 + 3 = 7$
$3 + 4 = 7$
$7 - 3 = 4$
$7 - 4 = 3$
2. $2 + 3 = 5$
$3 + 2 = 5$
$5 - 2 = 3$
$5 - 3 = 2$
3. $4 + 1 = 5$
$1 + 4 = 5$
$5 - 1 = 4$
$5 - 4 = 1$
4. $5 + 3 = 8$
$3 + 5 = 8$
$8 - 5 = 3$
$8 - 3 = 5$
5. $2 + 7 = 9$
$7 + 2 = 9$
$9 - 2 = 7$
$9 - 7 = 2$
6. $4 + 2 = 6$
$2 + 4 = 6$
$6 - 2 = 4$
$6 - 4 = 2$
7. $5 + 2 = 7$
$2 + 5 = 7$
$7 - 2 = 5$
$7 - 5 = 2$
8. $4 + 5 = 9$
$5 + 4 = 9$
$9 - 4 = 5$
$9 - 5 = 4$
9. $5 + 1 = 6$
$1 + 5 = 6$
$6 - 1 = 5$
$6 - 5 = 1$

Answer Key (cont.)

Page 163 *Writing Fact Families*
1. $2 + 3 = 5$
   $3 + 2 = 5$
   $5 - 3 = 2$
   $5 - 2 = 3$
2. $4 + 5 = 9$
   $5 + 4 = 9$
   $9 - 5 = 4$
   $9 - 4 = 5$
3. $1 + 2 = 3$
   $2 + 1 = 3$
   $3 - 2 = 1$
   $3 - 1 = 2$
4. $2 + 7 = 9$
   $7 + 2 = 9$
   $9 - 7 = 2$
   $9 - 2 = 7$
5. $3 + 5 = 8$
   $5 + 3 = 8$
   $8 - 3 = 5$
   $8 - 5 = 3$
6. $1 + 8 = 9$
   $8 + 1 = 9$
   $9 - 8 = 1$
   $9 - 1 = 8$
7. $2 + 4 = 6$
   $4 + 2 = 6$
   $6 - 4 = 2$
   $6 - 2 = 4$
8. $3 + 4 = 7$
   $4 + 3 = 7$
   $7 - 4 = 3$
   $7 - 3 = 4$
9. $3 + 6 = 9$
   $6 + 3 = 9$
   $9 - 6 = 3$
   $9 - 3 = 6$

Page 164 *Coin Purses*
1. 7 cents
2. 11 cents
3. 30 cents
4. 28 cents
5. 31 cents
6. 27 cents
7. 54 cents
8. 41 cents

Page 165 *Toy Store*
1. $14¢ + 8¢ = 22¢$
2. $9¢ + 14¢ + 8¢ = 31¢$
3. Tic-Tac-Toe and Jacks
4. $10¢ - 9¢ = 1¢$
5. Tic-Tac-Toe for 7¢ or Jacks for 8¢ or Jump Rope for 9¢
6. $7¢ - 5¢ = 2¢$ You need to save 2 more cents.

Page 166 *Pay For It*
1. one nickel
2. two dimes **or** one dime and two nickels
3. one quarter and two pennies **or**

two dimes, one nickel, and two pennies
4. one dime and three pennies **or** two nickels and three pennies
5. one quarter, one nickel, and two pennies, **or** two dimes, two nickels, two pennies
6. one nickel and two pennies
7. two quarters and two pennies **or** one quarter, two dimes, one nickel, and two pennies
8. one dime, one nickel, and two pennies

Page 167 *Two Different Methods*
Students' answers may vary. Suggested possibilities are shown below.
2. 1 dime, 1 penny **or** 2 nickels, 1 penny
3. 1 quarter **or** 2 dimes, 1 nickel
4. 2 quarters **or** 5 dimes
5. 1 nickel, 1 penny **or** 6 pennies
6. 1 dime, 1 nickel **or** 3 nickels
7. 2 dimes, 1 penny **or** 1 dime, 2 nickels, 1 penny
8. 4 dimes **or** 1 quarter, 1 dime, 5 pennies

Page 168 *Months of the Year*
1. January — 31 days
2. February — 28 days/29 days in a leap year
3. March — 31 days
4. April — 30 days
5. May — 31 days
6. June — 30 days
7. July — 31 days
8. August — 31 days
9. September — 30 days
10. October — 31 days
11. November — 30 days
12. December — 31 days

Page 169 *Reading a Calendar*
1. February
2. 28 days
3. Monday
4. 4
5. Tuesday

Page 170 *About How Long?*
1. hours
2. seconds
3. minutes
4. hours
5. seconds
6. hours
7. minutes
8. seconds
9. minutes
10. minutes

Page 171 *What Time Is It?*
1. 7:00 A.M.
2. 7:30 A.M.
3. 8:00 A.M.
4. 12:30 P.M.
5. 2:30 P.M.
6. 4:00 P.M.
7. 5:30 P.M.
8. 8:00 P.M.

Page 172 *Telling Time*

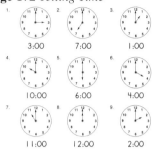

3:00   7:00   1:00
10:00   6:00   4:00
11:00   12:00   2:00

10. Answers will vary.

Page 173 *How Much Time?*
1. 30 minutes
2. 1 hour 30 minutes
3. 30 minutes
4. 1 hour
5. 1 hour
6. 30 minutes

Page 174 *Inch, Foot, or Yard?*
1. an inch
2. a foot
3. a foot
4. a foot
5. an inch
6. a yard
7. an inch
8. a yard
9. an inch
10. a foot

Page 175 *Using a Ruler*
1. 7"
2. 6"
3. 4"
4. 1"
5. 5"
6. 2"

Page 176 *Leafy Measurement*
1. 5 cm
2. 10 cm
3. 8 cm
4. 16 cm
5. 3 cm
6. 5 cm

Page 177 *A Pound, More or Less*
1. less than 1 pound
2. more than 1 pound
3. more than 1 pound
4. more than 1 pound
5. less than one pound
6. more than one pound
7. less than one pound
8. more than one pound
9. less than one pound
10. less than one pound
11. more than one pound
12. more than one pound

Page 178 *Heavy and Light*

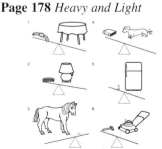

Page 179 *Measuring Tools*
1. calendar
2. scale
3. ruler
4. clock
5. cup

Answer Key *(cont.)*

Page 180 *Create a Clown*
Students' drawings may vary slightly. Ensure they followed the directions on the page in their drawing.

Page 181 *Create a Picture*
Students' drawings may vary slightly. Ensure they followed the directions on the page in their drawing.

Page 182 *Shape Riddles*
1. circle
2. rectangle and square
3. triangle
4. hexagon
5. square, pentagon, hexagon, triangle (as drawn)
6. pentagon
7. square, rectangle
8. rectangle

Page 183 *Identifying Solids*
1. cylinder
2. rectangular prism
3. cube
4. cone
5. sphere
6. pyramid
7. rectangular prism
8. cone
9. sphere
10. cylinder

Page 184 *Lines of Symmetry*

Page 185 *Draw Equal Parts*

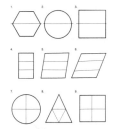

Page 186 *Name the Fraction*
1. 1/3
2. 2/4 or 1/2
3. 3/4
4. 2/3
5. 4/4 or 1
6. 3/3 or 1
7. ?
8. 2/5

Page 187 *Coloring Fractions*

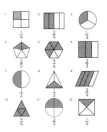

Page 188 *Sort By Attribute*

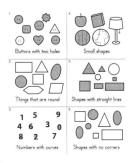

Page 189 *Sorting Shapes*
Students' answers will vary. Ensure they sorted the shapes in a consistent manner.

Page 190 *Extend the Pattern*

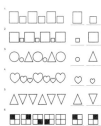

Page 191 *Create a Pattern*

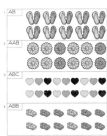

Page 192 *Number Patterns*
1. 5, 6, 7
2. 11, 16, 22
3. 18, 22, 26
4. 20, 18, 16
5. 32, 64, 128
6. 50, 40, 30
7. 33, 32, 31
8. 55, 50, 45

Page 193 *Count the Animals*
1. (cow: 3 tally marks)
2. (horse: 4 tally marks)
3. (chick: 10 tally marks)
4. (sheep: 5 tally marks)
5. (pig: 7 tally marks)
6. (cat: 3 tally marks)

Page 194 *Graphing Books*

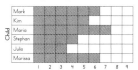

1. Maria   3. Julio
2. 2   4. Marissa and Mark

Page 195 *Graph a Fish Bowl*

Page 196 *Using a Bar Graph*
1. soccer   3. 1
2. 3   4. Answers will vary.

Page 197 *Problem Solving*
1. First—Mark
   Second—Sarah
   Third—Tony
2. Jose needs to buy 12 balloons.
3. Marice will need to pack his lunch 4 days.
4. Brenda would earn 50 cents.

Page 198 *More Problem Solving*
1. Each girl would get 4 pieces of candy.
2. Sean would have to buy 3 packs of gum.
3. Mary is 7 years old.
4. Emily spends 100 minutes walking to and from school each week.

Page 199 *What Would You Do?*
Sunny Day – Have a picnic, wear shorts, go to the park, climb a tree
Rainy Day – Use an umbrella, stomp in puddles, wear rain boots, float leaves in the water

Page 200 *Dress for the Weather*
1. mittens   4. jacket
2. swimming suit 5. cap
3. umbrella   6. shorts

Page 201 *Different Types of Houses*
1. stilts   5. motor home
2. stucco   6. apartment
3. igloo   7. adobe
4. log cabin   8. houseboat

Page 202 *Compass Rose*
1. North   5. North-East
2. North-West   6. East
3. West   7. South-East
4. South-West   8. South

Page 203 *Directions Quiz!*
1. North, South, East, West

Answer Key (cont.)

2. North is the opposite of South.
   East is the opposite of West.
3. North South West East
4.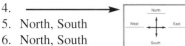
5. North, South
6. North, South
7. East, West
8. East, West

Page 204 *Which Way Should We Go?*
1. Take 3 steps south.
2. Take 4 steps east.
3. Take 2 steps north.
4. Take 2 steps west.
5. Take 1 step north.
6. Take 4 steps east.
7. Take 4 steps south.
8. Take 6 steps west.
9. Take 3 steps south.
10. Take 4 steps east.

Page 205 *Map Symbols*
1. airport   5. school
2. park   6. road
3. railroad   7. factory
4. river   8. hospital

Page 206 *You Make the Key!*

Page 207 *North, South, East, or West*
1. East   3. South   5. North
2. West   4. North   6. South

Page 208 *Your Map*

7. Answers
   will vary.

Page 209 *Continents and Oceans*
Continents—North America, South
America, Europe, Asia, Africa,
Australia, Antarctica
Oceans—Indian Ocean, Pacific Ocean,
Atlantic Ocean, Arctic Ocean

Page 210 *Our Country's Neighbors*

1. The United States
2. Canada
3. Mexico

Page 211 *The Pledge of Allegiance*
flag, America, republic, nation, liberty,
justice
nation—country
republic—government run by citizen
vote
liberty—freedom
justice—fairness

Page 212 *George Washington*
1. 1732
2. general
3. first
4. Washington
5. "Father of our Country"

Page 213 *Abraham Lincoln*
1. 1809   4. freed the slaves
2. books   5. Answers will vary.
3. 1860

Page 214 *The United States Flag*
1. red, blue   4. stripes
2. blue   5. thirteen
3. fifty, state

Page 215 *National Symbols Riddles*
1. Pledge of Allegiance
2. Mount Rushmore
3. Statue of Liberty
4. The Star-Spangled Banner
5. U.S. Flag
6. Bald Eagle

Page 216 *Martin Luther King, Jr.*
1. leader   6. laws
2. 1929   7. I have a dream
3. fairly   8. prize
4. minister   9. holiday
5. Coretta   10. dream

Page 217 *Timeline of My Life*
Students' answers will vary.

Page 218 *Long Ago and Today*
Long Ago—telephone, covered wagon,
camera, quill, butter churn
Today—CD player, computer, electric
car, cell phone, refrigerator

Page 219 *Goods and Services*
1. good   7. service
2. service   8. good
3. good   9. service
4. service   10. service
5. service   11. good
6. good   12. service

Page 220 *States of Matter*
1. gas   6. solid

2. liquid   7. gas
3. solid   8. liquid
4. liquid   9. gas
5. solid   10. liquid

Page 221 *Matter*
1. Matter   5. container
2. described   6. Solids
3. forms   7. shape
4. wet   8. spread

Page 222 *Plant Parts*
1. flower   4. seed
2. leaf   5. roots
3. stem

Page 223 *What Parts Do We Eat?*
1. root   7. flower
2. flower   8. leaf
3. root   9. stem
4. leaf   10. flower
5. root   11. root
6. seed   12. stem

Page 224 *Plant Part Functions*
1. seed   5. leaves
2. grow   6. stem
3. roots   7. Leaves
4. plant   8. flower

Page 225 *What Kind of Animal?*
1. mammal   5. insect
2. insect   6. reptile
3. fish   7. reptile
4. bird   8. mammal

Page 226 *Animal Body Coverings*
1. hair   7. feathers
2. feathers   8. scales
3. hair   9. scales
4. feathers   10. hair
5. scales   11. hair
6. hair   12. feathers

Page 227 *Animal Features*
1. fur, milk
2. feathers, fly
3. skin, eggs
4. Fish, gills
5. segmented, exoskeleton

Page 228 *The Water Cycle*
1. evaporation
2. condensation
3. rain
4. run-off

Page 229 *Describing the Water Cycle*
1. ocean   5. clouds
2. sun   6. rain
3. evaporates   7. runs off
4. condenses   8. water cycle